**LITERARY THE
FOR THE F**

**THE GUIDES FOR THE PERPLEXED SERIES**

# LITERARY THEORY: A GUIDE FOR THE PERPLEXED

## MARY KLAGES

continuum

Continuum International Publishing Group
The Tower Building                    80 Maiden Lane
11 York Road                          Suite 704
London SE1 7NX                        New York, NY 10038

First published 2006
www.continuumbooks.com

© Mary Klages 2006

All rights reserved. No part of this publication may be reproduced or
transmitted in any form or by any means, electronic or mechanical,
including photocopying, recording, or any information storage or retrieval
system, without prior permission in writing from the publishers.

Mary Klages has asserted her right under the Copyright, Designs and
Patents Act, 1988, to be identified as Author of this work.

**British Library Cataloguing-in-Publication Data**
A catalogue record for this book is available from the British Library.

ISBN: 0-8264-9072-7 (hardback) 0-8264-9073-5 (paperback)


**Library of Congress Cataloging-in-Publication Data**
A catalog record for this book is available from the Library of Congress


Typeset by Servis Filmsetting Ltd, Manchester
Printed and bound in the United States of America

# CONTENTS

CHAPTER 1

# WHAT IS 'LITERARY THEORY?'

Chances are, if you've picked up this book and are reading this introduction, you already have some conception about 'literary theory,'
and you want to know more. You've come to the right place. I teach
a course at the University of Colorado called 'Introduction to
Literary Theory,' and this book comes out of that class. It's meant
for anyone who has heard of poststructuralism or postmodernism,
or Derrida or Foucault or Lacan, and has wondered what those
words mean or who those people are, and why they are important.
It truly is a 'guide for the perplexed,' an attempt to help you out of
the dark tangles of theoretical doublespeak and into a world where
the ideas of 'theory' begin to make some sense.

This book is for those who know enough to be 'perplexed' by literary theory, and, to put it bluntly, for those who are frightened of
it. The students who appear in my class on the first day certainly are.
The course is required for all English majors, and we (the faculty)
want students to take it in the first or second year of college, so that
they are familiar with using these ideas and frameworks when they
reach their advanced literature courses. But most students put it off
until their final year because they've heard that the course is really
difficult, that it's more about abstract philosophy than about literature. They're scared that they won't 'get it,' and they don't even know
what 'it' is.

I start my course by asking students, on the very first day of class,
what they think a course called 'Introduction to Literary Theory' is
going to cover. I get responses ranging from 'I have absolutely no
idea' to 'it's going to introduce us to theories about literature,' which
amounts to the same thing. It's an unfair question, like asking you
to tell me the plot of a book you haven't yet read. That's also the

problem with the title of this chapter: 'What is Literary Theory?' We can try to come up with some basic definitions, and perhaps agree upon some sets of principles or rules that these theories use in analyzing literature – but we'll probably end up with ideas that are too vague and confusing to be of any real use. It's hard to say what 'literary theory' is until you already know something about what we mean when we say 'literary theory.' So this chapter asks a question we won't really answer.

Once we've established that we can't yet say what 'literary theory' is, I ask my students if they've ever read a work of literature. As you might imagine, everyone's hand goes up – after all, they are English majors! Of course they've read a work of literature! Most of them laugh at the question. But the laughter stops when I ask the next one: 'How did you know?'

We know some works qualify as 'literature' and some don't; not every printed book is 'literature.' If you go into a bookstore, probably there will be different sections organizing the books, and one of them will be something like 'Literature,' or 'Fiction and Literature,' which differentiates the category of 'literature' from all other kinds of printed texts. So what's the difference? What makes a text suitable to be placed in the 'Literature' section and not in, say, 'Self-help' or 'History?'

This gets us into a discussion of what we mean by 'literature,' and we start listing ideas in order to see how slippery a category 'literature' becomes when you try to pin it down. Is 'literature' confined only to fiction, drama, poetry, and essay, or can other kinds of writing qualify? Does it have to be written down? Printed? Published or shared? How do the bookstore workers know what books to put in the 'literature' section?

Most books say somewhere what category they fall into; on the back cover or on the copyright page there will usually be a Library of Congress or British Library listing that tells librarians and bookstore workers where the book should go. But who decides the category in which any book will be placed? On what basis, according to what criteria? Getting frustrated by the lack of definitive answers to these questions, you might point out that you know what books are 'literature' because someone in authority, usually a teacher, has told you that these are the books that are worth reading and spending time discussing. 'Literary' texts, perhaps, have more *value* than other kinds of texts. But then of course we have to talk about what we mean by 'value.' Is Shakespeare more 'valuable' than a plumbing manual? How do we decide what 'value' a text has? What is the 'value' of the texts we call 'literary?'

You might think of the touchstones that supposedly differentiate 'good literature' from mere fiction: that literature has withstood the test of time, that it speaks to all generations, and tells universal truths about human nature. I like to point to a scene in *Star Trek IV: The Voyage Home*, which came out in 1986. Captain Kirk and Mr Spock have traveled back in time from the twenty-third century to the late twentieth century (in order to save their civilization from certain destruction, of course) and are riding on a bus in San Francisco. They see passengers reading Danielle Steel and Harold Robbins, and Spock turns to Kirk and whispers, 'Ah. The classics.' This line always gets a big laugh. How can the schlock supermarket fiction of our time be thought of as 'classic literature' in the future? This scene tells us, however, that what we judge as 'valuable' 'literature' now might not be immutable and timeless, because standards of literary value and evaluations of literary excellence change over time.

The point of all of this is not to come up with some agreed-upon definition of 'literature,' nor to list all the ways we have of distinguishing 'literature' from other kinds of texts. Rather, I want my students – and you, my readers – to see that we all have assumptions about what makes literature 'literature.' These assumptions, whatever they might be, constitute our theories about what literature is, what it does, and why it's important.

In this sense, 'literary theory' isn't something you learn, it's something you become aware of. You already have a theory, or several theories, about literature, but you may have never thought about them or articulated them. And that's pretty much what this book is about: working to articulate, to understand, some of the basic assumptions we have about the category we call 'literature,' and about how a 'literary' text is – or isn't – different from any other kind of text.

Literary theories have existed as long as literature has. 'Literary Theory,' with the capital letters, points to sets of ideas that have greatly influenced the way we have thought about, taught, and produced scholarship on 'literature' within colleges and universities in the past 30 to 40 years. 'Literary Theory' is a big umbrella term that covers a variety of approaches to texts ('literary' or not); if these approaches have anything in common, it is that all of them examine factors that shape how a text is written and how we are able to read it. 'Literary Theory' comes from all kinds of disciplines, including linguistics, psychology, anthropology, philosophy, history, economics, gender studies, ethnic studies, and political science; much of what falls under the heading 'Literary Theory,' as you'll see, has little to do directly with what we think of as 'literature.'

Since it seems difficult to come up with a precise definition of 'literary theory' as a single graspable entity, perhaps we need to ask a different question. Why is 'literary theory' something important for students of literature to know? Why is 'literary theory' considered a necessary and valuable part of a literary education?

By way of answering this, let me tell you about my own experiences with 'Literary Theory.' I was an undergraduate English major from 1976 to 1980, just at the point when literary studies was shifting radically as a scholarly discipline. As an English major, I learned some essential skills, particularly that of close reading – learning to read a text carefully, word by word, in order to answer the question 'Why did the author choose this particular word, phrase, sentence structure, paragraph structure, image, symbol, meter, rhyme, etc.?' We started with the often-unstated assumption that every element of a poem, story, play, or novel had a purpose and a reason for being there, and that our job as students, as future literary critics, was to figure out that purpose and name those reasons. So I learned the technical skills for reading poetry, for example, recognizing metrical forms, being able to detect variations in meter and rhythm, and to extract some meaning from those variations; I learned the history and development of poetic and prose styles and forms, so that I could recognize what time period a work came from, and understand the conventions of that period or style or form.

In fact, I learned two old styles of being an English major. At my college in the USA, I learned how to do close readings of texts, to form my own opinion, give my own interpretation, in answering the question 'Why is this here?' In doing so, I learned skills of argument and explication, writing essays that had a clear thesis and strong supporting evidence taken directly from the text itself. Then, as part of my major, I spent six months at University College London doing the first-year English curriculum. This curriculum was organized very differently than my US English major. I attended lectures on seventeenth-century English literature, and met weekly with a tutor who assigned an essay topic relevant to the lectures, which I then prepared for the next week's tutorial. My tutor always asked me to research what literary critics had said about a particular work; my essay was to summarize what I found and offer some critique of the critics' opinions, either agreeing or disagreeing with someone else's viewpoint.

In the US major, I read nothing but original literary texts, and wrote about what I found there; in the UK major, I focused on reading what critics had said in order to be able to read the original literary text more carefully. In neither major did anyone ask me to ask *why* these skills and pursuits were valuable or important, or to think about anything outside of the literary text and its history and criticism. While my UCL tutor was impressed by my ability to have original thoughts and interpretations of literary texts (due to my US training), my US professors were impressed, on my return, by my thorough knowledge of literary history and criticism, something which had been made secondary, in my college's major, to the perfection of skills in close reading and argumentation.

And then I got to my senior year, spring of 1980. Just a few weeks before my graduation, I went into a bookstore and bought two recently published works in my field of interest, which was women writers and feminist literary criticism. The first was Sandra Gilbert and Susan Gubar's *The Madwoman in the Attic*; I took it home and read it avidly, feeling delighted that I had received an education solid enough to enable me to understand their arguments about 'the anxiety of influence' and about British literary history and the difficulties faced by women authors in the nineteenth century. The other book, however, baffled me. It was *New French Feminisms*, a collection of essays by feminist theorists like Hélène Cixous and Luce Irigaray and Julia Kristeva. Though the essays were in English, they might as well have been in a totally foreign language, as they talked about the Phallus and the Symbolic and the category 'woman.' I had no idea what they were talking about, or even what perspective or premise they were writing from. After ten pages, I threw the book across the room, yelled several expletives, and declared, 'I've been studying all the wrong things!'

And in some ways I had been. I had been studying 'literature': classical works of proven timeless value, their history, and what important critics had said about them. The authors of the essays in *New French Feminisms* were examining language, gender, and the unconscious; they were making references to Freud and Marx, to anthropology and linguistics, and to people I'd never heard of, like Lacan and Derrida.

This was a world-shattering – or world-*view*-shattering – moment in my intellectual life. I suddenly saw a world of thought of which I knew absolutely nothing, a realm of ideas which illuminated how 'literature' worked, but which my English major training had never mentioned. I didn't know it at the time, but I was experiencing the disorientation and confusion that my whole generation of literary scholars would go through in the next ten years, as the old methods of literary study were expanded and challenged (though never fully replaced) by this new thing called 'Theory.'

In graduate school, I encountered my first formal courses in 'Theory,' and even then they were partial and underdeveloped. I fought my way through Lacan, Derrida, and Foucault (without, I have to add, the benefit of any guidebooks like this one!) in the years when these thinkers' works were gaining attention in US academic circles, and their works were being translated into English and taught (albeit selectively and sometimes reluctantly) in university classrooms, at least at the graduate level. Slowly, painfully, I began to get a glimmer, first of what these theorists were actually saying (since 'deciphering' their dense theory-speak was like learning a foreign language itself), and then of why they were saying it, and what their assumptions and premises were. By the time I completed my doctorate, I was fairly fluent in 'theorese,' and by then a familiarity with the various branches of 'Literary Theory' had become a requirement for professional employment in an English department.

I'm telling you this to reassure you that I remember very vividly what it's like not to know 'Literary Theory,' and to find its intricacies perplexing and frustrating. I'm also telling you this as part of explaining why 'literary theory' is so ubiquitous in literary studies in the early decades of the twenty-first century. It's because of people like me, who were assaulted by the radical shift in the ways we thought about, talked about, and approached literature, from literary history and close reading to formulating ideas about texts based on theories 'outside' of literature, like linguistics and psychoanalysis. It's also because of a generational political awareness: the theorists like Foucault and Derrida, whose works have become the cornerstones of literary theory, were formulating their ideas in the context of the radical politics of the 1960s, in the USA as well as in Europe; the intellectuals and academics who began to read and teach their works in the USA in the 1970s were also products of that same political period. Their students, like myself, inherited many of the concerns of the 1960s, including political awareness of inequalities of race, gender, sexual orientation, physical ability, and the like, and these concerns, as articulated and addressed within the theoretical frameworks we were studying, became part of the questions we asked of literary texts in doing literary analysis.

So what do we do when we use literary theory these days? Well, I used to ask 'Why is this word here?' in analyzing a poem or story. Nowadays I still start with 'Why is this word here?' but my answers have more to do with 'What does this word do, how does it function, what does it produce?' than with 'What does it mean?' I still base my readings of literature (and of every other kind of text) on the skills of close reading I learned – that part of literary studies seems to me essential – but I no longer stop asking questions when I've explicated a passage of text and understood its grammar and imagery. I now spend more time asking 'What does this word/image/text do?' than asking 'What does it mean?'

I like thinking about literature as 'doing' something, rather than just 'being' something; it helps me understand literature as part of a larger world, rather than as a self-contained unit removed from real life. Literary texts, like all other kinds of texts, produce the world we live in, and 'Literary Theory' is a tool – or, better, a set of tools – which enables us to examine *how* that happens.

I want to bring up one more question about 'Literary Theory' in today's university curriculum before we move on to talk about what these theories actually say and do. When I was in graduate school, I was on a panel of professors and students who were making a pitch to wealthy alumni to make donations to the university; I was there to speak about the value of the English department, and I talked about how studying literature puts one in touch with core human values, and makes one a better person – standard rhetoric which I had learned as an undergraduate and which was what most of the audience, I suspect, expected to hear from a student defending her chosen field. But one man raised his hand and asked, 'What do you make? What's your *product*?' This question left me speechless. I could see his point: the engineering department makes engineers, who make stuff – bridges, electronic circuitry, space capsules. But the English department? What do we make? What do we produce? Somehow the answer that we make enlightened educated human beings seemed inadequate to the scope of the man's question.

I've spent many hours chewing on this question. I start, of course, by questioning the question: Why does the English department, or any university department, have to 'make' anything besides educated people? What kind of world-view prompts the questioner to assume that every discipline or department has to 'produce' something tangible or measurable? Part of what literature, and the humanities in general, is supposed to do is to foster the intangibles, the immeasurable values of life, the beliefs and forms of art without which life would be lifeless equations and bare facts. The humanities traditionally house the values that make life worth living, that make existence more than mere material survival and progress, that by definition can't be measured or quantified. But the man's question still echoes for me: in a world ruled by monetary economic concerns, what do English professors get paid for? What do English majors buy with their tuition? And how do we understand ourselves as part of an economic system that needs to persuade wealthy donors that they should give their money to us?

What my knowledge of literary theory tells me, 25 years after my college English major, is that my English department does indeed make something, produce something. Every academic deparment does: we make knowledge. Specifically, in the English department we produce knowledge about literature, in culturally sanctioned forms like essays of literary criticism and books of literary history – and theory. So what is this knowledge? Who makes it, who evaluates it, who uses it, and for what? Why is the study of literature still something that the university and its donors, the students and their tuition-paying parents pay for?

These are the kinds of questions that 'Literary Theory' helps us answer. We will still – probably always – be concerned with close reading and asking of a text 'What does this mean?' but we will also be concerned with 'How does it mean, what does it produce, and what effect does that have on us and on our world?' That's what 'Literary Theory' ultimately is about.

And that's why it's important to understand. Not just because your teachers think you ought to know this, but because these theories illuminate some basic assumptions we have about the world, and illuminate some of the basic mechanisms that work in our world to generate what we call 'meaning' – which is not limited to a 'literary' text. What we call 'Literary Theory' really ought to be named something like 'world theory' or just 'how things work,' because the theories that explain how meaning is made and what it produces are theories that explain how our everyday world works. And that, it seems to me, is something worth knowing.

So, at the end of the first day's class I tell my students to hold on! Be prepared to have your mind blown, to question everything, to enter into a world-view, a way of thinking, that will feel uncomfortable and unfamiliar at the least, and possibly profoundly disturbing. You're about to enter a perplexing landscape of ideas which will help you see things as you've never seen them or thought about them before. But relax. You have an experienced guide with you. I've taught 'Literary Theory' to about a thousand students over the past ten years, and every single one of them survived – and, I hope, understood.

# CHAPTER 2

# HUMANIST LITERARY THEORY

What I learned to do with literature in college didn't have any particular name; close reading and interpretation, analysis and argument were simply what one did with literature if one was an English major. Similarly, we didn't ask *why* we studied literature (although our parents, and sometimes our peers, did). The answers were obvious, and had been taught to us all through school: literature, and art in general, what we call 'the humanities,' makes us better human beings, puts us in touch with human values and dilemmas, helps us understand the human condition.

The Literary Theory I studied in graduate school came from an entirely different set of assumptions and premises. In fact, the Literary Theory with which most of this book is concerned starts by asking tough questions of those ideals, and working to understand where these ideals have come from. In graduate school, I learned that these notions, which had always gone unnamed, taken for granted, in college, actually had a label: they were *humanist* beliefs, and the theories that informed them were *humanist* theories.

Since so much of the Literary Theory we're exploring in this book comes from thinkers picking holes in humanist theory, it's worth our while to spend a chapter exploring what 'humanist' theory is, or has been, and how it came to shape the study of literature, and of all the disciplines belonging to 'the humanities,' up until about 1970.

'Humanism' is one of those words – literary theory is full of them – that lacks a precise definition, largely because its meaning varies depending on the context in which it appears. In broad philosophical terms, 'humanism' is a world-view or perspective that rejects anything supernatural as an explanation for existing phenomena. Rather than seeing the world as governed by some sort of divine spirit, like a god, which is the source of and reason for every-thing that happens, humanism argues that what we can observe with our senses can be explained by human investigation and thought. This view, as you might guess, forms the basis for what would become in the Western world the concept of 'science,' the idea that observation and deduction are sufficient means for understanding how the world works and how things happen, without reference to any kind of divine or extra-human power.

Since the latter half of the nineteenth century, historians and cul-tural critics have argued that the dawn of humanism marked the end of the medieval period and the beginning of the Renaissance, the flowering of art, literature, and science, from which we frequently date the beginnings of our modern culture. These historians claimed that, during the Renaissance, the rediscovery of Greek and Roman classical texts sparked the dawn of a new era in thinking. They saw the 'umanisti' – professional teachers and scholars in fourteenth- and fifteenth-century Italy who revived the study of Greek and Latin, rhetoric, logic, and mathematics as the basis of higher edu-cation – as the founders of the kind of high school and university curriculum on which the idea of the 'liberal arts' education was founded. These topics formed the basis for 'the humanities' as a dis-cipline, and distinguished humanities from 'divinities,' or the study of religious texts and doctrines.

While late-twentieth-century historians now see this as the effort of nineteenth-century scholars to project their own values and world-view onto the events of the Renaissance, what remains is the idea that the values of 'humanism' are central to the ways in which Western Anglo-European culture understands its own history, in terms of individual achievement, the power of rational thought, and the authority of science. In the broadest sense, humanism is the world-view that posits human values and concerns, rather than divine or supernatural values, as the central focus of life and thought. Because humanist thought displaced the idea of God as the absolute center of the universe, replacing it with the idea of the human mind as a supreme power of knowledge and creation, it is sometimes referred to as 'secular humanism.'

There are lots of arguments and debates about what humanism is, and whether it's a good thing or a bad thing, especially around the teaching of so-called 'humanist' values in public schools. The Suggestions for Further Reading will direct you to some sources for further exploration of these debates. For our purposes, it's more important to look at the ideas which form the basis for humanist thought, for the disciplines known as 'the humanities,' and for humanist literary criticism. Once we have a sense of where 'humanism' comes from and what its basic assumptions are, the structuralist and poststructuralist responses to and critiques of humanism will make more sense.

Like just about everything in Western Anglo-European culture, we'll start with Plato.

## PLATO (c. 427–347 BCE)

The ancient Greeks had literature, but not literary theory, until Plato came along. Ancient Greek literature included epic and dramatic poetry, comedy and tragedy, and perhaps some other forms of story-telling. These forms were presented orally, through characters who acted out human situations and thus provided models for human behavior and interaction. In ancient Greece, cultural knowledge was passed on via a tradition of presentation, or representation – by telling or acting out stories. There was, however, no way to distinguish between types of stories: between history, mythology, biography, and what we know call fiction.

Plato founded a philosophic tradition in which reason, the human capacity for rational thought, became the highest and most desirable form of thought, and the preferable means for conveying cultural knowledge. Reason, for Plato, was a process of logical deduction, as demonstrated in his Socratic dialogues; stories, poetry, and drama, because they appealed to their audiences' emotions more than to their rational minds, became inferior methods for passing on cultural values and demonstrating the best ways of being. For Plato, art, because it aroused the emotions, could never be 'true' in the way that reasoned argument could be true. Truth, for Plato, could only be apprehended through rational thought, as exemplified in mathematics, particularly in geometry, where eternally perfect formulae for generating figures (such as the area of a right triangle) could be derived from a handful of basic premises.

Plato's preference for reason over emotion, and for the truths of mathematics over the 'truths' of human feeling, came in part from his insistence that reality resided in forms that were eternal and unchanging, rather than in the chaotic and ever-shifting material world where human beings lived. Plato, and all Platonic philosophical systems that followed him, imagine the world that we can perceive with our physical senses – the world we can touch, smell, see, hear, and taste – as an illusion or a reproduction of another realm, a more perfect world, which is the world of the ideal. In this realm, things exist in their most perfect form, and never change; their static condition makes them eternal and therefore the source or essence of all the things that exist in our human material world. Objects in our world are merely copies of the forms that exist in the ideal realm and, because they are copies, they are necessarily less perfect than their original forms. According to Plato, we can understand the world of forms      you can substitute the words 'truth,' 'essence,' and 'ideal' here as well – only through reason and the process of logical argument

Philosophers use logic and reason to discover truth. Artists, by contrast, evoke emotions by making representations of the world we can perceive through our senses. For Plato, all art was representational; whether in words or colors, poetry or painting, art created pictures of the material perceivable world, which Plato called 'nature.' But since 'nature' was itself only a reproduction, a copy, of what existed in perfect form in the realm of the ideal, any art that reproduced nature was merely copying from a copy. For Plato, an artist's work was always twice removed from the world of truth and ideal perfection. And, because artists worked to stimulate emotions in their work, rather than, like philosophers, to train rational powers, artists were also associated with the irrational, with madness, and with the forces that were potentially dangerous and disruptive to the processes of logic and rationality.

Because of this double threat – because their creations were copies of copies, and because these copies excited feelings rather than reason – Plato worried that art and artists might threaten social order, because they might distract citizens from the pursuit of the eternal truths which were the only unfailing source of goodness. In Book X of the *Republic* Plato points specifically to poets and poetry in warning that 'all poetic imitations are ruinous to the understanding of the hearers, unless as an antidote they possess the knowledge of the true nature of the originals.'[1] Though Plato in other dialogues tries to salvage poetry by urging poets to write about the lives of exemplary statesmen to encourage citizens to emulate their virtues, in the *Republic* he reluctantly but firmly banishes all poets as too dangerous to remain in his ideal society.

Plato worried that art, including literary art like poetry and drama, tells lies and influences its audience in irrational ways. His concern with the content of literature begins a tradition in literary criticism and theory which focuses on the effect that literature has on its reader or audience. This tradition of moral or didactic criticism argues that literature is so powerful a medium for arousing emotions, without necessarily presenting any rational assessment or tempering of those emotions, that it can present a constant danger to its audience, especially when that audience consists of the 'weak-minded' or least rational of a society's citizens – women and children, for example. Moral criticism focuses solely on the content of a work of literature, asking whether its effect is good or bad, rather than paying attention to its artistic or formal values.

It is worth noting, for future reference, that Plato establishes some of the most fundamental and influential ideas in Western thought, ideas that structuralist and poststructuralist literary theorists wrestle with constantly. These include the ideas that

- the material world we perceive through our body and our senses is not the real world, but an imperfect copy of an ideal world
- art, in whatever form or medium, works to reproduce or represent the perceivable material world
- what is excellent and beautiful and right and good is that which approaches, through rational processes, the truth of the ideal form
- the world is organized into pairs of binary opposites: rational/irrational, good/evil, male/female, public/private
- literature is important, and needs to be regulated or supervised, because it has a powerful effect on its readers
- the content of literature, what it says and represents, is more important than the form it comes in.

### ARISTOTLE (384–322 BCE)

The other ancient Greek 'founding father' of Western thought, by contrast, is less interested in the content of literature than in its forms. Plato begins his literary theory by remarking in passing on the place of poets and poetry in his *Republic*, while Aristotle's *Poetics* is the first full work in the Western tradition devoted specifically to literary criticism. To understand Aristotle's views on poetry and poetics, it is useful to start by understanding how Aristotle understood the nature of reality, the material world, and the human perception of reality, and to see how Aristotle's views contrasted with Plato's.

Aristotle begins with the idea that art is not necessarily an imitation or a reproduction of nature, of the world we perceive with our senses, and thus is not necessarily an inferior reproduction or copy of nature. Rather, for Aristotle, art is a process of putting the events of nature into a medium (such as words or paint) that improves on or completes nature. Art doesn't lie, according to this view, but reveals truths in a different way than rational deduction. For Aristotle, art is not necessarily the binary opposite of reason, and thus threatening to logic and rationality; Aristotle understands that the pleasure we take in representations conveys another type of 'truth,' not a disruptive and dangerous falsehood.

For Aristotle, 'reality' does not reside in a static eternal world of perfect ideal forms, in relation to which the material world is a flawed imitation; rather, reality is the ever-changing world of appearances and perceptions, the ordinary world of things and events. Within this ever-changing world, 'form' appears only in concrete instances. Whereas Plato thought that any particular chair was only an imitation, an inferior copy, of the ideal form of 'chair' that could not be perceived directly through our senses, but only deduced by logical processes, Aristotle, by contrast, argues that the only way we can know the essence of 'chair,' the true meaning of 'chair,' is through individual instances of chairs. For Aristotle, form exists only in the concrete examples of that form, not in some eternal ideal abstraction. In the world we perceive through our senses, things exist according to ordered principles which we can discover; Aristotle's 'truth,' what his philosophy seeks to understand and teach, resides in discovering the rules and principles that govern how things work and take on meaning in our material world.

As you might be able to tell from this description, Aristotelian thought forms the foundations for science in Western philosophy. Aristotle is interested in observing specific phenomena (like watching how someone sits down in a particular chair) and then deducing from those observations the rules that govern how all chairs behave (such as the principle that all chairs must have some sort of seat to support a person's bottom). Aristotle's science desires to catalog and classify the things of the material world; his methods work to discover similarities and differences in form, and to deduce general principles of organization, or taxonomy, from these forms, rather than in the specific operation of any individual. Aristotle's science is the foundation for biological classification systems as we know them: if you learned in high-school biology how to classify an organism by placing it within the system of kingdom, phylum, class, order, family, genus, and species, then you learned an Aristotelian system of organization.

Aristotle treats poetry, and all art forms, like biology: he is interested in discovering or creating ways to identify characteristics of various forms of poetry and then developing systematic categories through which to classify these forms. While Plato founds the tradition of moral criticism by worrying about what a work of poetry does to its audience, Aristotle founds the tradition of *genre* criticism by investigating what a particular work *is*, rather than what it does. Aristotle's *Poetics* examines literature in terms of its internal structure; it focuses on drama, working to identify the formal properties of comedy and tragedy. Comedy, according to Aristotle, must deal with 'base' people, with peasants and average folk, while tragedy must confine itself to the lives of the nobility. Aristotelian criticism is interested in discovering the essential qualities of each of the different kinds or forms of literature, and then determining how and in what proportion all the elements of any particular form should come together to form one unified literary work.

For Aristotle, the artist does not imitate nature, or copy it, as Plato argued, but rather takes something from nature and puts it into a different medium that it doesn't inhabit in its natural state. Think, for instance, of a cherry tree. A cherry tree exists as a concrete object in the natural world, and we can classify it according to its similarities to and differences from other kinds of trees. An artist comes along and paints a picture of the cherry tree, or writes a poem about it; he or she is not just copying the tree, but actually creating a new version of the cherry tree, through the process of putting it in a new medium. By re-presenting the cherry tree in colors or words, the artist makes the tree over, re-creates it. Aristotle's artist is not just an imitator, then, but also a creator, and this ability to create gives artists a more important role in Aristotle's world than the suspect one they have in Plato's *Republic*.

Artists are important, to Aristotle, because art imposes order on what might otherwise be a disordered and chaotic natural world. Just as scientific observation and the formulation of general rules and principles that explain the phenomena of the material world create order, rationality, sense, out of what would otherwise be seen as random events, so art makes order out of the myriad sensory experiences we have every day. Literature in particular imposes a particular kind of narrative order on events, so that what is described in words has a beginning, a middle, and an end. For Aristotle, art and literature thus complete a process that the natural world leaves incomplete; nature merely presents us with events, phenomena, sensory experiences (like the sight of a cherry tree in bloom), while art, by creating an order in which to understand those events and experiences, provides us with their *meaning.* Thus art and literature are positive social forces, according to Aristotle, rather than the dangers that Plato feared; rather than just arousing emotions which threaten a citizen's love of reason, Aristotle's artists create order and system, and help citizens find pleasure in the representation of an understandable and meaningful reality.

With Plato and Aristotle we see the emergence of the two most fundamental strands or traditions in Western thought about art and literature: the concern with the content and effect of a work of art, and the concern with the form and unity of a work of art. The first, following Plato, might be called moral criticism; the second, following Aristotle, could be broadly labeled formal or aesthetic criticism. Most subsequent critics, well into the twentieth and twenty-first centuries, tend to follow one strand or the other. What follows is an overview of what various theorists have added to or amended in Plato or Aristotle from the beginning of the Common Era through to the end of the nineteenth century.

## HORACE (65 BCE–8 BCE )

Quintus Horatius Flaccus, more commonly known as Horace, was a Roman poet, best known for his satires and his lyric odes. His letters in verse, particularly his *Ars Poetica: Epistle to the Pisos*, outline his beliefs about the art and craft of poetry. His main contribution to the traditions of literary theory we are exploring lie in his articulation of the purpose of poetry, or literature in general: it is *dulce et utile*, sweet and useful. Horace insists that literature serves the didactic purpose which had been Plato's main concern, and that it provides pleasure; the two goals are not incompatible, as Plato had feared. Poetry is a useful teaching tool, Horace argues, precisely because it is pleasurable. The pleasure of poetry makes it popular and accessible, and its lessons thus can be widely learned. Like Plato, Horace sees nature as the primary source for poetry, but he argues that poets should imitate other authors as well as imitating nature. Horace thus establishes the importance of a poet knowing a literary tradition, and respecting inherited forms and conventions, as well as creating new works.

Except for a few late Roman and early medieval writers who contributed to the discussion of theories about literature, such as Plotinus (204–70), Boethius (480–524), St. Thomas Aquinas (1225–74), and Dante Alighieri (1265–1321), the writings of Plato, Aristotle, and Horace pretty much defined the parameters of thought about literature from the ancient world until the Renaissance. The explosion of art, literature, and science which we think of as the hallmark of the European Renaissance in the fourteenth to the sixteenth centuries prompted not only a deluge of literary texts, including the works of such luminaries as Shakespeare, but also a torrent of writings about the purpose, form, and importance of literature. The Renaissance discourse on literary theory was stimulated at least in part by the rediscovery of Aristotle's *Poetics*, a text which had been lost to Western culture during the Dark Ages.

### SIR PHILIP SIDNEY (1554–86)

England, although it could boast an important emergent literary tradition starting in the Middle Ages with Chaucer, didn't make any significant contribution to literary theory until the second half of the sixteenth century, when Sir Philip Sidney wrote *An Apologie for Poetrie* in 1583. His impassioned defense of poetic art came as a response to an attack on poetry by a Puritan critic who followed Plato in arguing that poetry was a waste of time, that it was based on lies, and that it taught sinful things. Sidney's discussion of poetry follows in the path laid out by Horace, insisting that the art serves the dual purpose of instruction and pleasure.

> Poesy therefore is an art of imitation, for so Aristotle termeth it in his word *mimesis*, that is to say, a representation, counterfeiting, or figuring forth – to speak metaphorically, a speaking picture; with this end, to teach and delight.[2]

Poetry, according to Sidney, provides a vehicle for instructing readers in the proper ways to be, think, act, believe, and do, just as much as sermons or histories, and it has the advantage over these drier forms of providing enjoyment while it teaches. He answers the Puritan accusations that poetry is 'the mother of lies' by following Aristotle's logic: if poetry were merely an imitation of nature, it would be necessarily an inferior copy, hence a form of falsehood; but if poetry is an act of creation, then it completes a process that nature leaves incomplete and partial by teaching us the inner meaning of the things and events of the external material world. The mimetic quality of poetry, rather than presenting an inferior world, in fact presents a higher level of reality; the 'speaking picture' tells us forms of truth that would not be available through the raw observation of nature unshaped by poetic form.

## SIR FRANCIS BACON (1561–1626)

Sir Francis Bacon, a contemporary of Sidney and Shakespeare, also follows Aristotle rather than Plato in insisting that poetry does not present an inferior imitation of the real world, but rather that it presents a world that is better than the one we live in. In *The Advancement of Learning* (1605) Bacon argues that history, fact, and reason are necessarily tied to human experience, and can only present the world as it is known to our senses. Rather than seeing our sensory perceptions, as organized by reason, as a higher form of truth, Bacon argues that imagination, unchained by the limitations of sensory perception or actual experience, can create realities not yet manifested. Since desire, hope, imagination, and fantasy are not tied to the physical laws of nature, Bacon says that poetry can present a 'feigned history,' which, far from being a dangerous 'lie,' can speak directly to the human soul, and not just to the rational mind.

> The use of this feigned history hath been to give some shadow of satisfaction to the mind of man in those points wherein the nature of things doth deny it, the world being in proportion inferior to the soul; by reason whereof there is agreeable to the spirit of man a more ample greatness, a more exact goodness, and a more absolute variety than can be found in the nature of things. Therefore, because the acts or events of true history have not that

magnitude which satisfieth the mind of man, poesy feigneth acts and events greater and more heroical . . . .

Far from being dangerous and subversive, Bacon concludes, poetry has 'some participation of divineness,' because it can and does 'raise and erect the mind, by submitting the show of things to the desires of the mind,' whereas reason by itself 'doth buckle and bow the mind unto the nature of things.'[3] Just as the soul is greater than the world, so the imagined reality of poetry is greater than the perceptible material world. Even more importantly, for Bacon, poetry is greater than rationality because reason can only observe the pre-existing material world, not alter it; poetry allows the mind to create its own worlds, and to rule over them.

## JOSEPH ADDISON (1672–1719)

In *On the Pleasures of the Imagination*, three essays in *The Spectator*, published in June 1712, Addison explores the question of how poetry creates pleasure. Like Plato, he is concerned with how a literary work affects its reader, though unlike Plato he is less concerned with the moral effect of a poem than with its aesthetic effect; he is interested more in how a poem 'delights' than in how, or what, it 'instructs.' Following the mental philosophy (or psychology) of John Locke, Addison describes two kinds of pleasure in imagination. Primary pleasure comes from the immediate experience of objects through sensory perception; secondary pleasure comes from the experience of ideas, from the representation of objects (in words or pictures) when those objects are not present. He distinguishes the powers of the imagination from the powers of reason, noting that while reason investigates the causes of things, imagination is content with experiencing them, either directly or through representations. The imagination is less refined than the faculty of reason, and provides pleasure from observation of the obvious, rather than from probing hidden causation; the pleasures of imagination are thus more easily acquired than those of reason, and are more widely available to untrained minds. Addison agrees with Sidney and Bacon that art is not just an imitation of nature, but an improvement on or completion of it; he points out that the secondary pleasure of imagination makes it possible for an experience which would be disagreeable in actuality to be represented in pleasurable form. The danger of art, in this logic, lies in its ability to make represented experience preferable to actual experience, though Addison cannot explain why mimesis, representation, is in itself pleasurable.

## EDMUND BURKE (1729–97)

Like Addison, Burke follows John Locke in starting with the idea that all human knowledge comes from sensory experiences; Burke describes 'imagination' as the capacity to create complex ideas through the combination of the simple ideas gathered through the senses. Imagination is a creative power that works in two ways: to represent images of nature in the manner in which the senses originally perceived them, and to combine these images in new ways. Burke insists that the imagination cannot achieve wholly original creations – it only combines and reshapes the sensory perceptions the mind receives – but imagination is not tied to the natural world. Art, for Burke, is not an imitation or copy of the natural world, but is itself a kind of (re)creation.

In *A Philosophical Inquiry into the Origin of Our Ideas of the Sublime and Beautiful* (1757) Burke argues with Plato's idea that the artist is merely a copier, making imitations of the natural world, and the critical standard that judges art on the accuracy of its imitation of an existing object. Burke suggests that the critical assessment of art should be based on the idea of *taste*, the conception of what one wants a representation to do. A shoemaker may want an accurate picture of a shoe, while a dancer may want a picture that gives a sense of the shoe's motion and liveliness, an emotional rather than a physical quality. Taste is a matter of 'sensibility,' according to Burke, rather than a question of reason and logic. Like Addison, he believes that sensibility is more common than reason, since reason requires education and training, but that sensibility can be developed to a greater or lesser degree in individuals. For Burke, different viewers get different kinds of pleasure from different kinds of mimetic representations. This view lends itself to questions of how a society can educate its citizens' sensibility or taste, as well as its logical capacity, in order to teach people to take pleasure in the highest forms of art.

## SAMUEL JOHNSON (1709–84)

Johnson's essay 'On Fiction,' appearing in *The Rambler* on March 31, 1750, marks the beginnings of literary criticism of forms other than poetry and drama. Discussions of fiction appear in the middle of the eighteenth century following the rise of the novel as an important literary form. Like other kinds of art, fiction depends on the idea of mimesis, presenting stories which imitate nature or real life; unlike poetry or drama, however, fiction depends on the principle of *realism*, presenting stories of individuals to readers as if these individuals were real people. The realism of fiction blurred the distinction between the imagined world of art and the real world of history and biography. Fiction also depended on using language that aimed for transparency; unlike poetic language, which called attention to itself as a creation, as art or artifice, rather than the language of common speech, the language of prose fiction worked to call attention to the reality of plot and character, and away from the work as an imaginative creation.

Johnson follows Plato in insisting that criticism of literature, especially fiction, has to be based on an assessment of its moral effect: what does the work do to the reader? Good art, in this view, is art that has a positive moral message; bad art has a bad message, encouraging readers to emulate negative or destructive behavior. Novels are potentially more harmful than poetry, because novels are the more realistic form, thus more easily believed or mistaken for descriptions of real life. The realism of fiction, according to Johnson, also ties the genre more closely to the actualities of human existence, because they do not contain 'the wild strain of imagination' of poets, and do not rely on supernatural or inexplicable events. Fiction comes from authors who have direct knowledge of human nature, gained through intercourse with other humans, rather than from writers closeted away from the normal world inventing impossible scenarios. Because a novelist copies easily recognizable events and characters, Johnson argues, any reader can judge the accuracy of the representation, and evaluate a novel according to that standard. Because they are accessible and realistic, novels appeal to a wide audience, and novelists are thus obliged to be aware of the power their creations wielded; novels are often read by the young and ignorant, Johnson warns, and have the power to lodge ideas firmly in unformed minds, so novelists must take care to choose noble subjects and positive morals. The rule of realism should be bent, according to Johnson, so that novels deviate from nature whenever it is necessary to present the proper outcome, where wickedness is punished and virtue rewarded.

Johnson argues that the ancient Greek and Roman writers presented the best models for any literary art. Those works which have withstood the test of time have proved themselves useful, rather than harmful, to generation after generation of readers, and thus any critic or writer must have a thorough knowledge of the classical literary tradition.

## SIR JOSHUA REYNOLDS (1723–92)

Sir Joshua Reynolds was an eighteenth-century painter. His *Discourses on Art*, published in 1797, though they focus on painting, present ideas about representation which were central to the discussions of literary aesthetics and criticism going on during this period. Reynolds follows Plato in arguing that the highest and soundest kind of art, and of criticism, refers to an eternal immutable nature of things, a kind of universal ideal common to all times and all forms of art. The purpose of criticism, then, is to discover the beauties or faults in particular works of art (and artists), with reference to this universal ideal. But, Reynolds laments, critics are mortal, and thus their assessments of art are subjective, not immutable or eternal. The solution to this problem, Reynolds concluded, is to try to discover the principles of human nature on which all forms of imaginative art (including painting and poetry) are founded, and then to shape a criticism, an aesthetic standard, based on those principles.

All arts, Reynolds proposes, have in common that they address the sensibility or imagination, as opposed to the rational faculty of the human mind; in art, unlike in mathematics, 'the imagination is here the residence of truth.'[4] A trained sensibility can intuit the truth in a process in which the steps or evidence on which a conclusion is based cannot be retraced; sensibility is based on one's collected, and collective, life experiences, rather than on the development of the skill of logical argument. Unlike reason, according to Reynolds, intuition happens with no conscious mental effort; one can't be trained to feel. However, he adds, it is part of a well-trained rational faculty to be able to judge when reason should give way to feeling, and the assessment of art requires the subordination of reason to sensibility.

Like Burke, Reynolds argues that painting and literature are not strictly mimetic or imitative, and that aesthetic evaluations cannot be based upon the accuracy of a representation. Indeed, direct imitations constitute the lowest style or level of art, for Reynolds, suitable only for uncultivated minds; the more accurate a representation is, the more obvious it is. Refined taste or sensibility is the product of education and practice and exposure to higher forms of art than just accurate imitations. Painting and poetry both try to gratify the natural human propensity to take pleasure in mimesis by means other than those supplied by nature; art adds something to nature that makes it do more than merely represent the natural world. Poetry, for example, uses an artificial language (such as hexameter or pentameter) to improve on the language of common people. The artificiality of art is part of its pleasure, according to Reynolds. The pleasure of poetry or painting comes from its appeal to sensibility and to the love of the kinds of order, congruence, coherence, and consistency that are evident in a created work and not evident in the natural world.

The 'great end' of all art, for Reynolds, is to make an impression on the human faculties of imagination and sensibility, not on the faculty of reason. 'The true test of all the arts,' and thus the basis for a universal standard of criticism, 'is not solely whether the production is a true copy of nature, but whether it answers the end of art, which is to produce a pleasing effect upon the mind.'[5]

## WILLIAM WORDSWORTH (1770–1850)

The critics and theorists from Sir Philip Sidney to Sir Joshua Reynolds broadly represent the thinking of the Age of Enlightenment, and its debates about the relative importance of reason and imagination. These critics insist that the ancient Greeks and Romans provide the best models for eighteenth-century art, that art is remarkable for its artifice and artificiality, and that the highest forms of art come from, and are appreciated most by, those with well-trained (classically-trained) sensibilities. William Wordsworth and Samuel Taylor Coleridge's *preface to the second edition of Lyrical Ballads* (1800) articulates the Romantic philosophical and aesthetic world-view. The Romantic conception of art and artists directly challenged the beliefs of the Enlightenment, particularly in insisting on the superiority of all things natural over anything artificial.

Wordsworth overturned centuries of accepted thought about poetry in stating that a poet is a 'man speaking to man,' and that poetry must use the language of common speech, rather than the artificial conventions of meter and rhyme which had been the hallmark of poetry since the ancient Greeks. The human interaction with the natural world provides the inspiration and source of all poetry, according to the Romantic view, and so the language used to present these interactions must work to re-create that naturalness. Wordsworth, and the Romantics in general, set up a value system in which the rural is valued over the urban, nature is better than culture, and the uneducated and simple are closer to nature than the educated and complex. In stating that 'the child is father of the man,' Wordsworth declares that children have a sensibility which adults have lost; children and other 'primitives' are especially endowed with a closeness to and a perception of unmediated nature which we lose as we become civilized adults – a loss which is necessary, inevitable, and tragic.[6]

Wordsworth is more concerned with the relation between the poet and the poem than with the poem and its reader; he is not particularly interested in the moral effect of poetry. He focuses on examining what a poem is, how it's made, and who makes it, rather than on what it does. A poem, he proclaims, is not the product of reason or of art and artifice, but is 'the spontaneous overflow of powerful feelings' which 'takes its origin from emotion recollected in tranquility.'[7] *Feeling* is thus established as the central element in a poem, more important than action, situation, character, or mimetic accuracy. The purpose of a poem is not to teach overtly, not to shape thought, character, or action, but to express and produce powerful emotion. From this, Wordsworth concludes, a poem is good insofar as it is an authentic expression of feelings generated in a natural setting.

The poet who can produce such authentic expression of feeling is a kind of superhuman being, a receptive soul, a creative genius who feels things more powerfully than the average person, and who has a heightened ability to express those feelings – not because of education or training, but because of an inborn innate ability that sets the poet apart from the rest of humanity. Obviously, in this Romantic view, feeling, sensibility, and emotion are more important capacities than reason and logic. Reason dissects and breaks up experience to analyze it, while feeling unifies it; the intellect can only grasp nature in pieces, while the imagination grasps it in its entirety.

## SAMUEL TAYLOR COLERIDGE (1772–1834)

Like Wordsworth, Coleridge insists that art in general, and poetry in particular, constitutes special modes of knowledge. While reason creates divisions and categories, art values the unity of subject and object, the union of human and nature. For Wordsworth, the artist's heightened sensibility sets him apart from the rest of humanity; Coleridge takes that separateness and elevates the artist to the status of a god, who can create worlds that have never before existed.

Coleridge's critical writings, including *On the Principles of Genial Criticism* (1814) and his *Biographia Literaria* (1817), emphasize the idea of organicism as central to the Romantic world-view. The language and form of poetry – its language and meter – have to arise organically, naturally, spontaneously, from the interaction of the poet and the natural world, rather than being the process of intellectual deliberation or imitation of classical authors. Form, in this view, is always something internal to the poem or work of art, rather than something imposed externally.

Because the form emerges from the interaction of the poet and the natural world, the poet is free to make his own rules about poetic expression, and to create his own forms unique to his particular experience. Poetry thus ceases to be governed by inherited rules about meter, and is freed from its imitative ties to a tradition of poetic precursors whose excellence has been proved by the test of time. Thus the idea of aesthetic quality, whether a work of art is good or bad, in the Romantic view depends not on any conception of conformity, either in the accuracy of a representation or to existing norms and conventions, but rather in the originality of the work, and in its ability to express and produce powerful emotions.

In investigating the organic principle of poetic composition, Coleridge also examines the faculty of the imagination, dividing it, like Burke, into a primary and secondary form. Primary imagination is the living power of human perception, the presence in each and every human soul of the divine spark of creative power which is the life force itself – or, as Coleridge describes it, 'a repetition in the finite mind of the eternal act of creation in the infinite *I am*.'[8] Primary imagination is unconscious, a universal given of human existence. Secondary imagination, by contrast, is the conscious act of creation; it enables the poet or artist to dissolve, dissipate, and diffuse sensory impressions in order to re-create, reorder, and unify them. Primary imagination is experience itself; secondary imagination is the ability to take experience apart and put it back together again in a new form.

## JOHN KEATS (1795–1821)

Keats's conception of poetry, as articulated in his letters to Benjamin Bailey and George and Thomas Keats in 1817, follows the Romantic path established by Wordsworth and Coleridge. Rational thought breaks the world into subject and object for the purposes of classification and analysis in the Aristotelian process known as 'science.' Sensations, empathic experiences, and poetry, however, break down the boundaries between subject and object and insist on the interplay between the two. Poetry and science, empathy and reason, are incompatible and oppositional, for Keats. The poet must possess a quality that Keats calls 'negative capability,' which is the ability to stay in, be comfortable with, uncertainties, indeterminacies, mysteries, and doubts without needing to find some resolution or certainty. Keats here articulates what would increasingly become a central conflict in literary studies in the twentieth century: formalist criticism would focus on finding a resolution or an explanation for the unity of elements in a poem, while poststructuralism would recall Keats's 'negative capability' and the need for ambiguity and flux, rather than answers.

## EDGAR ALLAN POE (1809–49)

Poe's critical writings, including 'The Poetic Principle' (1849) and 'The Philosophy of Composition' (1850), represent Romantic ideas of poetry taken to an extreme. Poe insists that a poet's only concern should be the concentrated effect of the work to produce an intense emotional response in the reader; a poem should be short, to be read in one sitting, so as not to interrupt this effect, and should have as its central concern the presentation of the most universal emotion, which he decides is grief over the death of beauty. Poe also rejects entirely the instructional or didactic aspect of poetry; its purpose is only to delight (or to arouse), not to teach or moralize. Poe thus becomes one of the earliest advocates of 'art for art's sake,' valuing poetry solely for its creation of feeling according to its own self-created internal coherence, without regard for any other external social effect or function that it might have.

## MATTHEW ARNOLD (1822–88)

Our last representative in this overview of literary theorists who have articulated the central premises of humanism is the critic most closely associated with the humanist perspective, and with the establishment of the humanities, and especially literary study, as a vital part of the high school and university curricula. In 'The Function of Criticism at the Present Time' (1864), Arnold states that the goal of criticism is 'to see the object as in itself it really is,' free of polemics, agendas, and preconceptions, in order to provide disinterested observation and assessment.[9] This is the heart of what would be called 'New Criticism,' the method of examining a literary text without reference to anything outside of the text itself. Critics who assess literature in this way will be able to make judgments about the quality of the literature itself, without promoting any particular agenda; this will enable them to find 'the best that has been thought and said' and to make those masterpieces known to the reading public. Familiarity with 'the best' literature has the power, according to Arnold, to create what he calls 'sweetness and light,' which are the hallmarks of civilization; the citizens who have been educated to appreciate 'the best' will develop taste, sensibility, a quality Arnold calls 'high seriousness,' and will be productive and peaceful members of their society. In short, Arnold tells us that a literary education in 'the best' texts will indeed make us all better human beings, and make our world an easier and more humane place to live.

These are some of the assumptions of the humanist world-view that led to the establishment of the 'liberal arts' education which is the basis for the twentieth-century college (and college-preparatory) curriculum. Matthew Arnold envisioned a high school and college education that would focus on training human beings to be fully human by insuring that they have exposure to the arts, sciences, and humanities. The study of subjects whose value had been established over time, which were known to contain, or to teach the path to, universal truths about the human condition, would free us from the preconceptions of our own era and connect us with what was eternal and immutable. The study of literature specifically would work to articulate the middle-class values of culture preached by Arnold, and make those values truly 'universal' by teaching them to all ranks of hierarchical British society.

When departments of literary study (more commonly known as English departments) began to take shape in British and American universities in the latter half of the nineteenth century, they encountered a problem of legitimacy. How could they ensure that trained professionals, with qualifications and degrees matching those of professors in the sciences, would be teaching students worthwhile lessons about literature? If the purpose of studying literature was to develop the taste, educate the sympathies, enlarge the mind, and improve the soul of a human being, how could those things be measured, tested, and graded? How could they be studied with the kind of rigor that made biology or philosophy a worthy academic subject? How could scholars insure that literary studies would be objective and disciplined, and not just based on an individual's likes and dislikes?

These forms of humanist literary theory all supported the emergence of a particular method of literary study, which was called 'New Criticism' or 'practical criticism.' The basis of this method lay in the practice of close reading: studying the text itself in close detail to discover its internal organic unity. T. S. Eliot, as well as other New Critics, argued that the analysis of the operations of the language of the text, to the exclusion of any other factors, including the author's biography, the historical context in which the work appeared, how it related to other works before, during, and after its appearance, and how critics and readers responded to the text, would place literary study on the same authoritative ground of objectivity as the sciences. Thus 'New Criticism' and close reading came to be simply, and often namelessly, 'what one did' in an English department – until about 1980, when I graduated from college and discovered that I had learned all the wrong things.

## NOTES

1 Plato, *The Republic*, Book X, in Hazard Adams, ed., *Critical Theory Since Plato*. New York: Harcourt Brace Jovanovich, Inc., 1971, p. 33.
2 Sir Philip Sidney, *An Apology for Poetry*, in Adams, ed., p. 158.
3 Sir Francis Bacon, *The Advancement of Learning*, in Adams, ed., p. 193.
4 Sir Joshua Reynolds, *Discourse XIII*, in Adams, ed., p. 370.
5 *Ibid.*, p. 375.
6 William Wordsworth, 'My Heart Leaps Up,' line 7.
7 William Wordsworth , *Preface to Lyrical Ballads*, in Adams, ed., p. 432.
8 Samuel Taylor Coleridge, *Biographia Literaria*, in Adams, ed., pp. 470–471.

9  Matthew Arnold, 'The Function of Criticism at the Present Time,' in Adams, ed., p. 584.

## SUGGESTIONS FOR FURTHER READING

Charles E. Bressler, *Literary Criticism: An Introduction to Theory and Practice*. Upper Saddle River, NJ: Prentice Hall, 2003.

Robert Cavalier, *Plato for Beginners*. New York: Writers and Readers Publishing Inc., 1990.

Tony Davies, *Humanism*. London: Routledge, 1997.

Richard Osborne, *Philosophy for Beginners*. New York: Writers and Readers Publishing Inc., 1992.

Dave Robinson and Judy Groves, *Introducing Plato*. New York: Totem Books, 2000.

Rupert Woodfin, *Introducing Aristotle*. New York: Totem Books, 2001.

# CHAPTER 3

# STRUCTURALISM

Structuralism is a way of thinking that works to find the fundamental basic units or elements of which anything is made. Structuralism takes its impetus from Aristotelian science, and more specifically from the developments in chemistry and physics in the nineteenth century that established that all matter was made of molecules, and that all molecules were made of atoms. While we now know that atoms themselves consist of many different kinds of subatomic particles, the atom is still thought of as the basic building block common to all forms of matter – everything in the universe is made of atoms. A structuralist analysis of a pencil, for instance, might look at how certain kinds of atoms combine in certain patterns according to certain rules to make the wood and graphite cylinder we write with.

Structuralism appears in a variety of disciplines or fields, including anthropology, linguistics, mathematics, and literary and cultural criticism. In any field, a structuralist is interested in finding the basic elements – the *units* – that make up any system, and in discovering the *rules* that govern how those units can be combined. And that's all. A structuralist analysis is not concerned with anything beyond the interrelationship of units and rules.

How does this work for literature? A structuralist view of a literary text would start by asking what are the most basic units, the 'atoms,' of a text. Well, a literary text, like any other kind of written text, is made of language, so a structuralist analysis of literature would start with a structural examination of language itself.

Linguistics was one of the first, and most important, disciplines to adopt a structrualist perspective, because the operations of any language fit well into a structuralist framework. All languages are made of units that combine according to rules to make meaning or sense. The basic 'atom' of language is the word (or, more strictly, the phonemes which make the sounds that make up words), and the rules are the forms of grammar which tell you how to put words together to make a sentence. In different languages the grammar rules are different, as are the words and phonemes, but the structure of language is the same everywhere: words are put together within a grammatical system to make meaning.

Part of the appeal of structuralism is that, like science, it reduces complex systems to their most fundamental parts. Also like science, structuralist analysis makes the claim to universality, to finding the structures or elements that are common to all cultures, at all times, in all areas of the world. The quest for 'universal' or 'timeless' truth, as we have seen, is central to the humanist world-view, and becomes problematic when the construction of 'universality' serves to mask or erase important differences between cultures, time periods, and belief systems. Structuralist analysis bypasses that problem by bypassing all questions of content: a structure can be universal, the same in all times and cultures, precisely because it is only a structure, a skeleton, a framework, on which specific individual content is built. From a structuralist perspective, all human beings would be fundamentally the same, because all share the same skeletal structure, regardless of what kind of skin or organs or brains might distinguish one particular occupant of a skeleton from another. From the same viewpoint, all languages are the same, because all have the same structure, regardless of what kind of words they contain.

If you've ever played a game called Mad Libs, you've seen the structure of language at work. Mad Libs players are asked to contribute a particular kind of word, a part of speech, such as an adverb, noun, verb, adjective, proper name, or exclamation, without knowing how those parts of speech will be used. One person writes down all the responses, then reads a pre-written story, using the parts of speech supplied by the players to fill in particular blanks within the story. The game might generate a sentence like this: 'My *noun past tense verb* the *adjective noun adverb*, which could be completed by players as 'My car kissed the blue table harshly.' The completed sentences always make grammatical, if not conceptual, sense because a noun always goes in the place where nouns go, verbs in the verb position, and so on. Whatever particular part of speech you supply, the structure of the sentence always remains the same.

Here's another example: I'll give you three characters and you tell me the story. The characters are princess, stepmother, and prince. Just about everyone comes up with 'Cinderella,' or other titles that tell pretty much the same story. From a structuralist point of view, Cinderella and Snow White are both the same story: the princess is persecuted by a stepmother and rescued (and married) by a prince. The 'units' here are the stock characters, and the 'rules' are that step-mothers are cruel, princesses are victims, and princes and princesses have to marry. Whatever details or added elements you supply, the basic structure of this story is always the same. And that's what structuralist analyses of literature, myth, or other kinds of narrative are interested in.

This kind of analysis has obvious limitations, as it seems the goal is to reduce all stories to some basic bare-bones structure and then see how all stories are structurally the same. This is, in fact, what some critics have tried to do; Vladimir Propp, and the Russian Formalists in general, hoped to find the 'atoms' of myth and literature by identifying the core components all myth had in common. Propp discovered some 31 functions present in the structure of all folk-tales, and showed that these functions were constant, regardless of the specific details of the individual folk-tales. This may not seem like a very productive or useful way to analyze literature; once you've identified the units and explained the rules, you're done, and there's nothing more to say. For those of us who are used to reading litera-ture in order to interpret complex webs of meaning, this kind of structuralist analysis is overly reductive and dehumanizing.

Structuralism sees itself as a 'science' of humankind, and works to uncover all of the structures that underlie all the things that humans do, think, perceive, and feel, in mathematics, biology, lin-guistics, religion, psychology, and literature. Structuralists believe that the mechanisms which organize units and rules into meaning-ful systems come from the human mind itself, which acts as a struc-turing mechanism that looks at units and files them according to rules. This means, for structuralists, the order we perceive in the world is not inherent in the world, but is a product of the organiz-ing capacity of our minds. It's not that there is no 'reality' out there, or that reality is beyond human perception, but rather that there is too much 'reality' – too many units of too many kinds – to be perceived coherently without some sort of 'grammar' or system to organize and arrange them.

This might resonate for you with some of the humanist ideas we explored in Chapter 2, including the idea that the natural world is incomplete or disorganized, and that art makes nature better by creating order and meaning from it; in structuralism, the human mind functions in the same way art does, to create an order that doesn't exist by itself. More importantly, though, structuralism has in common with humanism the belief in some kind of universal human characteristic or activity. Structuralist analysis posits the capacity of the human mind to create organizing systems as a cultural universal, and sees the structures created as fundamentally the same in all times and in all places. For example, every human culture has some sort of language, and every language has the same basic structure: words or sounds are combined according to a grammar of rules to produce meaning. Every human culture similarly has some sort of social organization, like a government, some sort of system for determining who can marry whom, usually referred to as a kinship system, and some sort of system for exchanging goods, called an economic system. All of these modes of organizing human life proceed, according to structuralist analysis, from universal structures.

## FERDINAND DE SAUSSURE

In this section we're going to look at the ideas Saussure brings forth in his famous *Course in General Linguistics*, which was published in 1916. Let's start by asking why we would be studying Saussure, a linguistics theorist, in our pursuit of literary theory. When we discard the assumptions of humanism, we start our new conceptions of how literature operates by noting that, first and foremost, literature is made of language. To understand how literature works, then, we must have some ideas about how language itself works. Saussure, as a structuralist, is interested in the universal structure of language; his ideas apply to any language – English, French, Farsi, computer language, sign language – and to anything we can call a 'signifying system.'

What's a 'signifying system?' Any set of units and rules that create a method for conveying meaning. Any kind of 'code,' such as Morse code or a 'secret' code, is a signifying system; so are typographical symbols, road and traffic signs, and referee hand signals in sports. A signifying system, regardless of how many elements it has, how simple or complex it may be, operates according to one of the fundamental principles of any language, according to Saussure, and that is the association of a word with an idea or thing.

In humanist theory, language is a transparent medium for naming things. Words perform the simple act of representing things, and various kinds of humanist linguistic theory have discussed how any particular thing gets associated with its word in a specific language. Saussure, and structuralist linguistics, complicates this view. The humanist view that words are linked to the things they name is useful, Saussure says, because it gets across the idea that the basic linguistic unit has two parts. Beyond that, however, structuralist linguistics abandons the humanist understanding that words get their meanings from the things they represent.

A linguistic unit, or *sign*, consists of two parts, which Saussure names the 'concept' and the 'sound image.' The sound image is not the same as the physical sound (what your mouth makes and your ears hear), but is rather the psychological imprint of the sound, the impression it makes. Think of talking to yourself 'in your head' – you don't make a sound, but you have an internal impression of what you're saying.

The linguistic sign is made of the union of a concept and a sound image. The union is very close, as one part will pretty much instantly conjure the other; Saussure's example is the concept 'tree' and the various words for 'tree' in different languages. When you are a speaker of a certain language, the sound image for 'tree' in that language will automatically conjure up the concept 'tree.' The *meaning* of any sign is found in the association created between the sound image and the concept; the sound 'tuh-ree' in English means the thing with branches, roots, and leaves. Meanings can, and do, vary widely, but only those meanings which a community or culture agrees upon will appear to name reality.

The linguistic sign is more commonly referred to as the combination of *signifier* and *signified*. The sound image is the signifier and the concept is the signified. You can think also of a word you say as a signifier and the thing the word represents as a signified (although technically these are called sign and referent, respectively).

The sign, as the union of a signifier and a signified, has two main characteristics:

1. The bond between the signifier (sfr) and signified (sfd) is *arbitrary*. There is nothing in either the thing or the word that

makes the two go together, no natural, intrinsic, or logical relation between a particular sound image and a concept. An example of this is the fact that there are different words, in different languages, for the same thing. 'Dog' is 'dog' in English, 'hund' in German, 'chien' in French, 'perro' in Spanish. If there was something inherent in a dog that generated the word that represented it, the word for 'dog' would be more or less the same in all languages.

This principle of arbitrariness dominates all ideas about the structure of language. It makes it possible to separate the signfier and the signified, or to change the relation between them. This makes possible the idea of a single signifier which could be associated with more than one signified, or vice versa, which makes ambiguity and multiplicity of meaning possible.

There may be some kinds of signs which seem less arbitrary than others. Pantomime, sign language, and gestures (which are often called 'natural signs') seem to have some logical relation to what they represent. Holding your nose to indicate contempt or dislike may seem logical, since you'd do that if you encountered a bad smell, but Saussure insists that *all signs are* arbitrary. The gesture of holding your nose only has meaning because a community has agreed on what that signifies, not because it has some universal or intrinsic meaning.

Saussure discusses at some length whether symbols, such as the use of scales for the idea of justice, are innate or arbitrary, and decides that these too are the result of community agreement. He also dismisses onomatopoeia (words that sound like what they mean, like 'pop' or 'buzz') as still conventional agreed-upon approximations of certain sounds. Think, for example, about the sounds attributed to animals. While all roosters crow pretty much the same way, that sound is transcribed in English as 'cock-a-doodle-do' and in Spanish as 'cocorico.' Interjections also differ from culture to culture. In English one says 'ouch!' when one bangs a finger with a hammer; in French one says 'Aie!'

As a structuralist, Saussure is not interested in how communities agree on establishing the relationship between signifiers and signifieds, nor is he interested in how those relationships might change over time. Structuralist analysis is always *synchronic*, meaning that structuralists look at a whole structure or system at the present moment, as if it had always been that way and would always be that way. Modes of analysis that try to account for changes over time, to look at the origins and evolutions of any system, are called *diachronic*.

2. The signifier (sound image, spoken word) exists in time, and that time can be measured as linear. You can't say two words at the same time and have both be intelligible; you have to say one word and then the next, in a linear fashion. The same is true for writing: you have to write one word at a time in order for each word to be distinct, and we conventionally write our words in a straight line.

This idea is important because all language operates as a linear sequence, and all elements of a particular sequence form a chain. Perhaps the most obvious example of the linearity and sequentiality of language is the sentence: words come one at a time and in a line and, though we read them individually we generate meaning through understanding that the words are all connected together.

Another fundamental premise in Saussure's conception of language is the idea that all thought takes place in the medium of language. Saussure conceptualizes thought alone as a kind of shapeless mass, which is only ordered by the structure of language. This question, whether ideas exist independently of their means of expression, has intrigued philosophers for centuries. According to Saussure, no ideas pre-exist language; language itself gives shape to ideas and makes them expressible, and thought cannot exist without language. In this sense, human beings don't speak language, language speaks us. For Saussure, sound is no more fixed than thought, though we can distinguish between different sounds, and thus associate a particular sound with an idea. Sounds thus serve as the signifiers for the ideas, which become their signifieds. In this view, signs (the union of signifier and signified) are always both material and physical (like sound) and intellectual (like ideas). Saussure insists that language is not a thing, a substance, but a form, a container, a system, a structure. He compares sound and thought, or signifier and signified, to the front and back of a piece of paper, which is the sign as a whole: you can distinguish between the front and the back, but you can't separate them and still have a piece of paper.

Saussure wants to focus our attention on the system of language as a whole, rather than on the individual parts of the system. Using the French word for language, he calls the system as a whole *langue*, and calls any individual part of language, such as a word, a *parole*. Structuralist linguistics is more interested in *langue* than in *parole*. The arbitrary nature of the sign explains why *langue*, language as a whole system, can only arise in social relations. It takes a community to set up the relations between any particular sound image and any particular concept to form specific *paroles*. That's what you do whenever you use any kind of language or code within a community context.

An individual can't say what a signifier/signified combination means – or, rather, you can make up your own private code or language, but you can't use it to communicate with anyone else unless someone else agrees on what signifiers go with what signifieds. As a structuralist, Saussure is not interested in how communities make agreements about associations of signifiers and signifieds. Other theorists of language, such as eighteenth-century philosopher Jean-Jacques Rousseau, focus on how these agreements come about.

We generally use the term 'meaning' to talk about how a signifier and signified come together. Saussure bypasses this term in order to distinguish between two ways in which what we call 'meaning' occurs. The connection established between any particular signifier and its signified he calls *signification*; signification exists on the level of the individual *parole*. Meaning is also produced within a structure as a whole, at the level of *langue*; Saussure calls this *value*, which is the relation between signs within an entire signifying system. As Saussure describes, 'language is a system of interdependent terms in which the value of each term results solely from the simultaneous presences of the others.'[1]

Saussure is saying that value comes from the fact that one particular term, or unit, is surrounded by all the other terms or units of a system. How does this happen? A good example might be money. A dollar bill is a signifier, but of what? The piece of paper is supposed to be the equivalent of one dollar's worth of gold – but that hasn't been true since sometime in the nineteenth century. But we all agree that the green bill is worth one dollar, just as we agree that the sound-image 'tree' signifies the thing with roots and bark and leaves. How is the bill worth one dollar? In Saussure's terms, how does the dollar bill have *value*?

Value can't be determined in isolation; a dollar bill doesn't have any worth unless it's part of a system of exchange. A dollar bill can be exchanged in two ways: you can trade it for something else that costs one dollar, like a cup of coffee, or you can trade it for something else that is worth one dollar, like four quarters or ten dimes. In either case, the bill has value, in Saussure's terms, only because it has a relationship to other elements in the system.

The most important relation between signifiers in a system, the relation that creates value, is the idea of *difference*. According to Saussure, one signifier in a system has value because it is *not* any of the other signifiers in the system. This is a tough but crucially important concept in structuralist and poststructuralist thought, so make sure you have a good grasp of it. Note Saussure's distinction between *signification* and *value*. Signification is a positive relationship, where a signifier is connected to one specific signified; this is the way we usually think about how language works, where a word designates a thing – or, in Saussure's terms, a sound-image designates a concept. In a relation of signification, meaning occurs because one thing (signifier) is linked to one other thing (signified) in a binary pair.

Value, by contrast, is a negative relation: we know what one signifier is because it's not any other signifier in the system. The word 'cat' has signification when it's connected to its signified, the animal that meows; the word 'cat' has value because it's not the word 'hat' or 'bat' or 'cut' or 'cap.'

You might think also about the letters of the alphabet in this context. The sound 'tuh,' made with the tip of the tongue against the teeth, is represented in English with the symbol 't.' Because the connection between sound and concept, or signifier and signified, is always arbitrary, that sound you make with tongue and teeth could just as easily be represented by another symbol, such as % or # (in which case we'd spell the thing that meows 'ca%' or 'ca#'). Connecting the sound with a symbol is signification. The sound of 'tuh' also has value because it is *not* the sound 'buh' or 'kuh.' We could create a signifying system where the sounds 'tuh,' 'buh,' and 'kuh' were symbolized by %, #, and &. It wouldn't matter which sound went with which symbol, as long as you could tell the difference between the sounds and between the symbols – as long as 'tuh' was different from 'kuh' and % was different from &. Another example of this might be the digital language recognized by computers, which consists of two switch positions, off and on, or 0 and 1. 0 has meaning because it's not 1, and 1 has meaning because it's not 0. That's the idea of value.

In the *Course in General Linguistics* Saussure explains further how the structure of signifying systems operates. Everything in the system is based on the relations that can occur between the units of a system, whether positive or negative, relations of signification or of value. There are also two ways or patterns in which units form relationships within a system: *syntagmatic* and *associative* relationships.

Syntagmatic relations are, basically, linear relations. In spoken or written language, words come out one by one, in a one-dimensional linear form. The words then form a kind of chain, in which one unit is linked to the next because they are in an order in a line. An example of this is the fact that, in English, word order governs meaning. 'The cat sat on the mat' means something different than 'the mat sat on the cat' because word order – the position of a word in a chain of syntagmatic relations – structures meaning. (You can also see the idea of value in operation in this sentence, since 'cat' and 'mat' and 'sat' are all different words.)

English word order has a particular structure: subject–verb–object. You can say the structure of English in one sentence: 'The adjectival noun verbed the direct object adverbially.' Other languages have other structures. In German, that sentence might be 'The adjective noun auxiliary verbed the direct object adverbially main verb.' In French it might be 'The noun adjective verbed adverbially the direct object.' In Latin, word order doesn't matter, since the meaning of the word is determined not by its place in the linear chain of the sentence, but by its case (nominative, ablative, etc.).

Combinations or relations formed by position within a linear chain (like where a word is in a sentence) are called syntagms. Examples of syntagms are any phrase or sentence that makes a linear relation between two or more units: 'under-achiever;' 'by the way;' 'lend me your ears;' 'when in the course of human events.' The terms within a syntagm acquire value only because they stand in opposition to everything before or after them. Each term is something because it's not something else in the sequence.

Syntagmatic relations are most crucial in spoken and written language, in *discourse*, where the ideas of time, linearity, and syntactical meaning are intertwined. There are other kinds of relations, however, that exist outside of discourse. Signs are stored in your memory, for example, not in syntagmatic linear chains, but in *associative* groupings. The word 'education,' for example, might get linked in your mind with other words that end in '-tion,' like relation, association, deification. You may store the word 'education' with words that evoke an experience you've had: education, teacher, text-book, homework, tuition. Or you may store words in what looks like some completely random set of linkages, but which makes sense to you: education, baseball, James Bond movies, guacamole (which is a list of things I like).

Associative relations are only in your head, not in the structure of language itself, or in any system outside your own mind. Syntagmatic relations are the product of the structure in which they exist. Syntagmatic relations are important because they allow neologisms to arise and be recognized and accepted in a linguistic community, such as the trend in 'verbing' nouns. Associative relations are important because they break patterns established in strictly grammatical (syntagmatic) relations and allow for the creation of new ways of linking units – or, what we in English call metaphors.

## CLAUDE LEVI-STRAUSS AND 'THE STRUCTURAL STUDY OF MYTH'

A signifying system can be any part of a culture that contains signs which can be 'read' and interpreted by determining signification (how signifiers are connected to signifieds) and by determining value (how one sign is different from all other signs in the system). This idea is at the heart of any kind of structuralist analysis. Saussure applies it to language; Claude Levi-Strauss, an anthropologist, applies it to kinship systems and other forms of cultural organization, including myth.

For Levi-Strauss, structuralist analysis offers a chance to discover the 'timeless universal human truths' so beloved of the humanist perspective, but using a methodology that seems much more objective and scientific. As an anthropologist, Levi-Strauss wanted to discover, at the level of structure, what all humans share by virtue of being human. One of the most basic structures shared by all human societies is kinship: every society that has ever existed anywhere has had some sort of system for deciding who can marry whom, who inherits what from whom, and how all of these relationships are named. Such a kinship system operates like Saussure's *langue*, containing units – in this case, men, women and children, who are labeled as fathers, mothers, sons, and daughters – and rules for connecting those units. In *The Elementary Structures of Kinship* (1969) Levi-Strauss points out two important functions of kinship systems.

The first is that kinship systems structure how goods, ideas, and people are 'exchanged' within a culture, giving form to that culture's economic, educational, religious, and social relations. He specifically notes that kinship systems explain what he calls 'the exchange of women,' wherein family groups 'give' a woman to another family to be a wife, and receive in exchange something of equal value, known as a bride-price.

More important to us now, however, is Levi-Strauss's insistence that the relations among units within the kinship system, or any structure, occur in *binary pairs*, which are either similar to each other or different from each other. This corresponds, in linguistics and literature, to the idea of metaphor and metonomy: metaphor is the establishment of a relation of similarity between two things (A is like B, or A is B), while metonomy is the establishment of a relation of contiguity, or closeness and difference, between two things. An example is saying 'crown' for 'king,' or 'sails' for 'ships.' The main point here is that relations between units in a system can only be analyzed in pairs: you know that A is A because it's not B, and A is A because it's not Q, and A is A because it's not %. You can only examine A in relation to one other unit of the system at a time, comparing A:B, A:Q, A:%. What's important to Levi-Strauss here is not the identity of any individual unit, any *parole*, but the *relation between any two units compared in a binary* pair.

Levi-Strauss's writings on kinship, culture, and myth often start to look like algebraic equations because of this focus on relational pairs. He uses as an example the idea of clans or totems within a tribal system, which are only comprehensible in structural relation to each other. A tribe may have a turtle clan and a hawk clan, but the practices of each clan are not related to the animal they're named after, but rather to the structural relationship between all possible clan animals. You can't understand the turtle and hawk divisions by thinking about how turtle people are like turtles and hawk people are like hawks; rather, you have to think about how the difference or relation between real turtles and real hawks are reproduced in the relations between turtle people and hawk people. If this were a mathematical problem, we'd call real turtles A, real hawks B, turtle people C, and hawk people D, and the structural relationship would be expressed as A is to B as C is to D, or A:B::C:D.

In *The Raw and the Cooked* (1969) Levi-Strauss discusses how binary pairs, particularly *binary opposites*, form the basic structure of all human cultures, all human ways of thought, and all human signi-fying systems. If there is a common 'human nature' or 'human con-dition,' from this perspective, it's that everyone everywhere thinks, and structures their worlds, in terms of binary pairs of opposites, like 'the raw and the cooked.' Even more importantly, in each binary pair one term is favored over the other: cooked is better than raw, good is better than evil, light is better than dark, etc. This idea is crucial both to Levi-Strauss's structuralist analysis of myth and to many of the poststructuralist ideas we'll be looking at in the rest of this book.

In his essay 'The Structural Study of Myth,' Levi-Strauss looks at another kind of human universal: the similarity of myths from cul-tures all over the world. He notices that cultures widely separated by geography or time still have distinctly similar myths explaining, for example, the creation of the world, the creation of language, the difference between the sexes, and other facts of human existence. Given that myths could contain anything – they are stories, not bound by rules of accuracy or laws of probability – why are so many myths from so many different cultures so much alike?

He answers this question by looking not at the content of each myth, but at their structure. While the specific characters and actions differ greatly, Levi-Strauss argues that their structures are almost identical. In making this argument, Levi-Strauss insists that myth is a language, because it has to be told in order to exist; we might add that myth is a language in the sense that any signifying system, as described by Saussure, can be called a language.

Myth, as language, consists of both *langue* and *parole*, both the synchronic, ahistorical structure and the specific diachronic details within that structure. Levi-Strauss adds a new element to Saussure's *langue* and *parole*, pointing out that *langue* belongs to what he calls 'reversible time' and *parole* to 'non-reversible time.' He means that a *parole*, as a specific unit or instance or event, can only exist in linear time, which is unidirectional – you can't turn the clock back. *Langue*, on the other hand, since it is simply the structure itself, which doesn't ever change, can exist in the past, present, or future. Think of the 'sentence' of English: 'The adjectival noun verbed the direct object adverbially.' If you read the sentence word by word, you read from left to right, one word at a time, and it takes a second or two to read the whole sentence: that's non-reversible time. If you don't 'read' the sentence, but see it as a whole, as the name of the structure of English, it exists in a single moment, every moment, yesterday the same as today the same as tomorrow. That's what Levi-Strauss calls reversible time, because it doesn't matter whether you go forward in time or backward in time: the structure, the *langue*, is always the same.

A myth, according to Levi-Strauss, is both historically specific, a kind of *parole* existing in non-reversible time as a story, and ahistorical, part of a *langue* that exists in reversible time as a timeless structure. He also says that myth exists on a third level, in addition to *langue* and *parole*, which also proves that myth is a signifying system of its own, and not just a subset of language. He explains that third level in terms of the story the myth tells. That story is special, because it survives any and all translations and variations. A myth can be altered, expanded, reduced, paraphrased, and otherwise manipulated without losing its basic shape or structure; you might want to think again about the example of 'princess, stepmother, prince' to see that, no matter what details you add to the story, the structure of relations among the units remains the same.

He thus argues that, while myth as structure looks like language as structure, myth is actually something different from language per se – he says it operates on a higher or more complex level. Myth and language both consist of units put together according to certain rules, and in both these units form relations with each other, based on binary pairs or opposites. But myth differs from language as Saussure describes it because the basic units of myth are not phonemes but what Levi-Strauss calls 'mythemes.' A mytheme is the 'atom' of a myth – the smallest irreducible unit that conveys meaning. Levi-Strauss's analysis of myth identifies the mythemes and then examines the sets or 'bundles' of relations among mythemes.

He thus creates for myth a two-dimensional structure, which allows for a different kind of 'reading' than the one-dimensional linear structure of language. Saussure's language is a line; one word is connected to the next in a grammatical structure. Levi-Strauss's myth, however, is like a square or rectangle: it has both a horizontal and a vertical dimension. Perhaps the best illustration of this shape is a musical score, with treble and bass clef. You can read the music for the melody, reading left to right, page by page, and you can read the music for the harmony, reading up-and-down, seeing the notes in the treble clef in relation to the notes in the bass clef. These two dimensions – the melody and the harmony, the horizontal non-reversible left-to-right way of reading and the vertical reversible up-and-down way of reading – are where Levi-Strauss finds his bundles of relations among units or mythemes.

Basically, a structuralist analysis of myth would first find the smallest component parts, the mythemes, which are usually one event or position or action in the narrative, the story, of the myth. Then the structuralist would lay these mythemes out so they can be read both horizontally and vertically, diachronically and synchronically, for 'plot' and for 'theme.' The story of the myth exists on the vertical left-to-right axis; the themes of the myth exist on the horizontal up-and-down axis. The relations formed by any two of the mythemes in this array constitute the basic structure of the myth.

In 'The Structural Study of Myth,' Levi-Strauss lays out the myth of Oedipus in this way, and sees in the synchronic (vertical) relations certain patterns, or what I've called 'themes,' developing. One such theme is the idea of having some problem walking upright; Levi-Strauss takes that theme and runs with it, seeing it as an expression of a tension between the idea of chthonic (literally, 'from the underground gods,' but here meaning 'having an origin in something external') and autochthonic (here meaning 'self-generated') creation. He then sees that tension, or structural binary opposition, as present in myths from other cultures. This, to Levi-Strauss, is the significance of the myth: it presents certain structural relations, in the form of binary oppositions, that are universal concerns in all cultures.

It may seem to you (as it does to me) that Levi-Strauss's analysis sounds a lot more like his interpretation of the myth rather than an objective reading of its universal structure. We might look at the Oedipus myth and come up with different interpretations for what he sees in the bundles of relations. For example, we might agree with him that one column focuses on ideas about walking upright. From that, we might see some fundamental anxiety about physical ability and disability, which is an expression of the tension between being fit for survival and needing charity and kindness; we could then read that tension (between selfishness and altruism) as the fundamental universal structure that the myth articulates.

So here's where you can start to see how this kind of structuralist reading might apply to a literary text. Once you've found the mythemes, the constituent units of a story, and laid them out in a two-dimensional grid, you can interpret them in an almost infinite number of ways. Your reading will depend on what you select as your mythemes and how you lay them out. This brings up the notion that maybe structuralism isn't as 'objective' and 'scientific' as it hopes to be, and that perhaps it is not uncovering universal human structures.

Levi-Strauss, in fact, wants to present structuralist analysis as very much a scientific method; in 'The Structural Study of Myth' he concludes that his method brings order out of chaos in the same way any scientific theory does, enabling investigators to account for widespread variations on the same structure. Structuralist analysis 'enables us to perceive some basic logical processes which are at the root of mythical thought,' and can 'provide a logical model capable of overcoming a contradiction.'[2] He refers here to contradictions like a culture's belief in two opposite things, like chthonic and autochthonic origins, or selfishness and altruism. Every culture has these contradictions, because every culture organizes knowledge into binary opposites, according to Levi-Strauss; myth helps reconcile these contradictions or opposites according to a discoverable logic.

Levi-Strauss insists that the 'logic' of structuralist analysis is just as rigorous as the logic of science. He wants interpretation to gain the same kind of cultural authority that scientific analysis has, and he thus invokes the mechanisms that give science its truth value: its logic and objectivity. One might critique Levi-Strauss's views by pointing out that his own argument sets up an opposition between science and myth, favoring science as the preferred method of truth, even as he asserts that myth is just as 'true' as science. But that's a deconstructive reading, not a structuralist one.

## NOTES

1   Ferdinand de Saussure, *Course in General Linguistics*, in Hazard Adams and Leroy Searle, eds, *Critical Theory Since 1965*. Gainesville, FL: University Press of Florida, 1986, p. 650.
2   Claude Levi-Strauss, 'The Structural Study of Myth,' in Adams and Searle, eds, p. 818.

## SUGGESTIONS FOR FURTHER READING

Paul Cobley, *Introducing Semiotics*. New York: Totem Books, 2001.
W. Terrence Gordon, *Saussure for Beginners*. New York: Writers and Readers Publishing Inc., 1996.
Donald D. Palmer, *Structuralism and Poststructuralism for Beginners*. New York: Writers and Readers Publishing Inc., 1997.
Boris Wiseman, *Introducing Levi-Strauss and Structural Anthropology*. New York: Totem Books, 2000.

# INTERLUDE: HUMANISM, STRUCTURALISM, POSTSTRUCTURALISM

Humanist criticism, which predominated in Anglo-American literary studies until challenged by structuralism and poststructuralism in the 1970s, shared fundamental assumptions about what literature was, how humans interacted with it, and why studying it was important. We can sum up these assumption in ten major points:

1.  Good literature is of timeless significance; it speaks to all generations at all historical periods.
2.  The literary text contains its own meaning within itself.
3.  The best way to study the text is to study the words on the page, without any predefined agenda for what one wants to find there.
4.  The text will reveal constants, universal truths, about human nature, because human nature itself is constant and unchanging. People are pretty much the same everywhere, in all times and all cultures.
5.  The text can speak to the inner truths of each of us because our individuality, our 'self,' is something unique to each of us, something essential to our inner core. However, each essential self shares certain universal constants with all other selves. The inner essential self can and does transcend all external social forces (so that, no matter what happens to me, I will always be me).
6.  The purpose of literature is the enhancement of human life and the propagation of humane values. Literature should, however, always be 'disinterested,' and should never have an overt agenda of trying to educate or persuade someone (which would be called propaganda).

7.  In a literary work, form and content are integrally and organically connected.
8.  A literary work is 'sincere,' meaning that it is honest, true to experience and to human nature, and thus can speak the truth about the human condition.
9.  Literature is valuable because it shows us our true nature, and the true nature of society, through pleasurable means, including drama, event, character, conflict, and symbolism. Literature shows us kinds of truth which science or other modes of inquiry cannot.
10. Literary critics interpret the text, based largely if not solely on the words on the page, in order to judge the quality of the literary text, as well as to show the reader how to read the text so as to get the most benefit from it.

All of the above should sound pretty familiar; these assumptions have been the basis for Western Anglo-European literary education through most of the twentieth century.

These points could also serve as a list of justifications for studying literature. From their beginnings, humanities programs, such as an English department, have had to explain their existence as academic disciplines by identifying, just like the sciences do, their proper object of study, the methodologies used to study it, and – increasingly in the latter half of the twentieth century – the goal or benefit provided to students, and to society at large, through pursuit of this area of study.

Structuralism offered one of the first serious challenges to humanist thinking because it proclaimed itself an objective and scientific mode of investigation. This made structuralism an attractive approach to disciplines which have been open to accusations of subjectivity and impressionism, including anthropology and literary studies. This objectivity is achieved by subordinating *parole* to *langue*, bypassing actual usage in favor of studying the structure of a system in the abstract. Structuralist literary theory ignores the specificity of actual texts and treats them as if they were like the patterns produced by iron filings moved by a magnet – the result of some impersonal force or power, and not the result of human effort.

In structuralist analysis, the individuality of the text disappears in favor of looking at patterns, systems, and structures, with the ultimate goal of discovering the universal structures that underlie all narratives. From this perspective, the author is canceled out, since the text is simply the function of a signifying system, not of an individual. The Romantic strand of humanism in particular held that the author is the origin of the text, its creator, and hence the starting point, the progenitor, of the text. Structuralism challenges this notion by arguing that any piece of writing, any signifying system, has no origin and that authors merely inhabit pre-existing structures (*langue*) that enable them to make any particular *parole*. Structuralism thus introduces the idea that we don't speak language, language speaks us. We don't originate language; we inhabit a structure that enables us to speak. What we (mis)perceive as our originality is simply our ability to recombine the elements within the system which exists before and beyond any individual human being. Hence every text, and every sentence we speak or write, is made up of the 'already written.'

By focusing on the system itself, in a synchronic analysis, structuralism cancels out history and the idea of change. Structuralists can't account for change or development; they are uninterested in how connections between signifiers and signifieds, for example, may have changed over time to produce new *paroles*. Most structuralists insist, as Levi-Strauss does, that structures are universal, therefore timeless; this is one of the reasons why structuralism, despite its anti-human stance, was appealing to humanist literary theorists.

More significantly, however, by erasing the author, the individual text, the reader, and history, structuralism represented a major challenge to the humanist tradition. Structuralism, and the poststructuralist theories which follow it, rely on a different set of philosophical assumptions than did humanism.

The humanist model presupposed that there is a real world external to our sensory perceptions which we apprehend through our physical senses and which we can comprehend with our rational minds. Language, from this perspective, is fundamentally representational: words can (more or less) accurately depict the real world and our experiences of it.

The (post)structuralist model, by contrast, assumes that the structure of language itself produces 'reality.' We can only think through language, and thus our perceptions and comprehensions of reality are all framed by and determined by the structure of language.

The humanist model held that language is a product of the individual writer's mind and free will. We determine what we say, and what we mean when we say it, and in that sense we are the creators of our own texts. Language thus expresses the essence of our individual beings, and can present the truth of our core essential selves.

In (post)structuralism language speaks us. The source of meaning is not an individual's experience or being, but the sets of oppositions and operations, the signs and grammars that govern the structure of language. Meaning doesn't come from individuals, but from the system that determines what any individual can do within it.

Finally, humanism held that 'the human' was the source and measure of all things; the world revolves, for humanist thinkers, around what human beings are and do and mean and say and produce and think and feel. Each human being has a 'self,' which is both unique to each individual and contains elements which are common or universal, part of 'the human condition.' This self is the core of our sense of identity, of who we are, as individuals and as part of any larger groups or cultures. The self is the center of all meaning and truth and knowledge, and language is the self's medium for unique expression of its perceptions, thoughts, and feelings.

(Post)structuralism counters this perspective by insisting that 'the self,' individual identity, is itself the product of the structure of language. The concept, and the utterance, 'I' only exists because 'I' is a signifier in the structure of language, and the signified attached to 'I' – what the humanists would call 'my self,' or 'me' – merely inhabits the structure of language and says 'I' to mark my subject position. For (post)structuralism, 'the human' is no longer the center; rather, 'the structure' becomes the source and shape of all meaningful activity.

Structuralism shook the foundations of humanism. The theories which followed structuralism critiqued and eventually discarded some of the assumptions and assertions of structuralism, replacing them with the ideas central to *poststructuralist* thought. The rest of this book will be exploring poststructuralist theories concerning language, the self, the construction of 'reality,' and the concept of 'truth.' Here, in a nutshell, are some of the ideas that these poststructuralist theories will address:

- Things that we have thought of as constant, including the notion of our own identity (gender identity, national identity, for example), are not stable and fixed, but rather are fluid, changing, and unstable. Rather than being innate essences, these qualities of identity are 'socially constructed' – and a lot of the theories we'll look at are concerned with *how* such identities are constructed so that they feel as though they are constant. Most poststructuralist theories throw out the idea that anything is absolute, especially any absolute truth, and instead focus on how everything is constructed and provisional.

- Everything one thinks or does is in some degree the product of one's past experiences, one's beliefs, one's ideologies; there is no such thing as objectivity. Where new critics, humanists, and even scientists claim that they can look at an object of study (like a literary text) with no preconceived notions of what they'll find, they are only masking their own ideological positioning. This idea relates back to the previous one, that truth is always relative, rather than absolute.
- Poststructuralist theorists agree that language is the most important factor in shaping our conceptions about life, ourselves, our world, and literary texts. Rather than language reflecting the 'real world,' language creates and structures everything we can know about 'reality.' Furthermore, rather than being speakers of language, we are products of language. Language speaks us.
- Because all truths are relative, all supposedly 'essential' constants are fluid, and language determines reality, there is no such thing as definitive meaning. There is only ambiguity, fluid meaning, and multiplicity of meaning, especially in a literary text.
- Because of the idea of relativism, there can be no such thing as a 'total' theory, one which explains every aspect of some event or field.

Having written that last point, I have to acknowledge that I've just listed these five premises of poststructuralism as if they were a 'total' theory, one that explains everything about poststructuralism. I'm writing here as if I still had the certainty and authority of humanism to say things as if they were unproblematically true. I've listed and defined them as if they were absolute, fixed, definitive, and total, instead of making you aware, through my writing style, of how provisional and ambiguous these poststructuralist ideas are. Poststructuralist theory is difficult because most theorists adopt a writing style that highlights the provisionality and ambiguity of meaning. They don't want to speak, or write, clearly, because to do so would be to affirm that there is such a thing as absolute meaning.

My job, for the rest of this book, will be to try to explain, clarify, and make comprehensible the ideas of some of the most important poststructuralist thinkers, even though their writings work against the possibility of explanation, clarification, and comprehension. As poststructuralist psychoanalyst Jacques Lacan insists, to 'understand' is to misunderstand; only when you think you don't get what these theorists are saying are you likely to be getting it, and vice versa.

Don't worry right now if you find all of this confusing: that's why you need this book. Don't worry too if you dislike all the ideas I've just described. Some people point to the decline of the humanist perspective, and the rise of poststructuralism as exactly what is wrong with the world today. If only we could return to the old-fashioned ideas, and believe in absolute truth, meaning, permanence, and the essential self, such people say, everything would be much better than it is now. Perhaps these people are right. What's important is not whether you like these theories, but that you understand what they say, and why they're saying it.

# CHAPTER 4

# DECONSTRUCTION

Deconstruction is a signifier that points to a complex and often confusing set of ideas, concepts, and practices. Jacques Derrida, the leading figure in deconstruction, insists that it is not a 'theory' per se, but rather a set of strategies or ways of reading. We can begin our exploration of deconstruction by noting that, first of all, Derrida and deconstruction come from an analysis of the history of ideas in Western philosophy, and offer a critique and alternative to many of the formulations which have been the philosophical foundations of humanist thought.

Structuralism takes 'the human' out of the center of analysis, as the cause and referent for everything, and replaces it with 'the structure;' structure becomes the most important element in any investigation, because the structure explains how all the units within it operate. Derrida takes this idea and applies it to Western philosophy, or Western metaphysics. He says that every philosophical system, every attempt to explain the relations among the mind, the self, and the world, posited some sort of *center*, a point from which everything comes and to which everything refers. In some philosophical systems the center is the concept of God; in others it's the human mind, or the unconscious, or space aliens, depending on whose system you're talking about.

This is the first thing that deconstruction adds to structuralism: all structures have a center. Note, however, that this model does not work very well for thinking about language; it's hard to see, once you take human beings away as a possible center, what could be the 'center' of the structure of language. So while we're exploring Derrida's ideas about the center, try not to use language as your example of a centered system.

## BINARY OPPOSITION

The second point that deconstruction makes comes from Levi-Strauss's insight that the units within a structure tend to group in binary pairs or oppositions, consisting of two terms placed in some sort of relation to each other. Derrida says that, within such structures based on binary pairs, one part of the pair is always given a higher cultural value than the other; one term is marked as positive and the other as negative. Hence in Western philosophy, we get pairs like good/evil, where good is preferable to evil. You might see how many binary opposites you can list in a single minute. The length of your list illustrates Derrida's point, that most of the ways we think about the world are structured into binary opposites.

Naming binary opposites will usually generate a fairly common list: it might include light/dark, day/night, up/down, right/left, male/female, white/black, etc. In Western metaphysics, the first term (the one to the left of the slash) is valued over the second term (the one on the right). And that's where the fun begins. We can, and do, argue about which term should be where. It's obvious that good is better than evil, but why is 'male' better than 'female,' or 'white' better than 'black?' That's exactly what deconstruction is asking. How is it that Western thought is structured primarily in terms of these binary oppositions, how is it that the first term is valued over the second, and (as you might guess from the word 'deconstruction') what would happen to the structure of Western thought if we took the binary opposites apart?

In his most famous work, *Of Grammatology*, Derrida looks specifically at the binary opposition 'speech/writing.' He argues that, in Western philosophy, speech has always been thought of as primary, or original, while writing is just a transcription of speech, or a copy of it. Derrida says that speech gets privileged over writing because speech gets associated with *presence* – for there to be spoken language, somebody has to be present and speaking.[1] The spoken word guarantees the existence of a person doing the speaking, while the written word doesn't necessarily point to a person who wrote it.

The binary opposition speech/writing thus correlates with the binary opposition presence/absence; speech and presence also point to the idea of the self, the speaker, as the origin of what is being said, while writing doesn't necessarily indicate who wrote it. The privileging of speech and presence over writing and absence, according to

Derrida, is an example of the *logocentrism* – word-centeredness – which is at the core of Western metaphysics (and hence of humanism).

Think for a moment about this line from Genesis: 'And God said, "Let there be light," and there was light.' That statement insures that there is a God (the thing doing the speaking) and that God is present (because speech = presence). The present God is the origin of all things, because God creates the world by speaking. What God creates is binary oppositions, starting with light/darkness. In this system (the world), God is the center and the creator of the structure of binary oppositions, within which everything that exists takes its place on one side or the other of the slash (/).

Think again of a list of binary oppositions, this time with philosophical concepts in mind: being/nothingness, reason/madness, word/silence, culture/nature, mind/body, self/other. Each term has meaning – Saussure's *value* – only in reference to the other, and only as what the other is not. Being is what is not nothingness, reason is what is not madness, word is what is not silence, etc. The binary opposites are inseparable in their opposition, because the term on one side of the slash only has meaning as the negation of what's on the other side of the slash.

Because of the favoring of presence over absence in Western thought, speech is favored over writing – and, as we'll see with Freud, masculine is favored over feminine because the penis is defined as presence, while the female genitals are defined as absence. I'll cover this in more detail in Chapter 5.

## THE ROLE OF THE CENTER

The structure of the binary opposition, and the fact that one side of a binary only has meaning in relation to the other side, to its opposite, means that every system posits a center, a place from which the whole system comes and which regulates the system. The center holds the whole structure in place, keeping each of the binary opposites on its proper side of the slash. Western philosophy has a great collection of terms that serve as centers to various metaphysical systems: being, essence, substance, truth, form, consciousness, human being, God, unconscious. Derrida tells us that each of these terms designating a center serves two purposes: it's the thing that is given credit for creating the system, the power that originated it and guarantees that all the units operate according to the rules, and it's also something beyond the system, not governed by the rules of the system itself.

In Derrida's conception of a structure, the center holds all the units in place, and in proper relation to each other; the center keeps the structure from moving very much. Derrida calls this kind of motion 'play.' The center limits the play of the structure, making it stable and rigid. You might think of a building as a structure. A central shaft might hold all the wings and floors of a building together, limiting how much the structure as a whole, and any single part of it, can move, in a tornado or hurricane, for instance. In a building, the lack of play is good. In a philosophical system or signifying system, Derrida says, it's not good.

You might also think of a kindergarten classroom. The teacher is the center. When he or she is there, the children behave – they act the way the center dictates. When the teacher leaves the room, the children go crazy, and 'play' wildly.

All structures and systems, including language, operate between two poles: absolute fixity, rigidity, no motion, no play, and its opposite, complete movement, constant shifting, continual play. Western culture, and Western philosophy, favors rigid systems over shifting systems, as it favors order over chaos, predictability over unpredictability, stability over shakiness. In linguistic terms, Western philosophy likes a single solid connection of signification – one signifier connected to one signified – better than ambiguity or multiplicity of meaning, where one signifier could have more than one signified, or vice versa. However – and this is a very important exception – Derrida's 'play' is precisely what makes literary language, especially poetic language, possible, since a single word can have more than one meaning.

This is where we can begin to see how these ideas about language and structure apply to 'literature.' What we call 'literary' are texts within which language tends to operate loosely, with lots of play. Non-literary texts, by contrast, use language as if meaning were fixed and stable. An example might be the word 'wrench.' In a poem, you can puzzle over the dimensions of meaning in the word; in a plumbing manual, you don't.

Derrida says that the center is the most important part of any structure. It's the point where you can't substitute anything. At the center, only the unit that *is* the center can be there; none of the other units of the system can take the place of the center.

For a philosophical or metaphysical system to illustrate this idea, you might think of early American Puritan culture. In the Puritan system of belief, God was the center of everything; anything that happened in the world (any event, or unit, of the system) could be referred back to God as the central cause of the event. And nothing in the system was the equivalent of God – nothing could replace God at the center as the cause of all things. Refer this back to Saussure's idea that units within a system form relations of exchange. The center of a system is something that has no equivalent value, nothing can replace it or be exchanged for it; it's the cause and ultimate referent for everything in the system.

The center limits play, and guarantees full presence; Derrida also refers to the center as a 'transcendental signified,' as the ultimate source of meaning, that which, paired with any and every signifier, creates the relation of signification which makes a sign able to say something. Because the center cannot be replaced by any other unit in the system, the center cannot be represented by anything else – it cannot become paired with just one particular signifier. You might think again of God as an example of a center; in some religions, God cannot be represented, in pictures or in words.

Because of this, Derrida says, the center is a weird part of any system. It's part of the structure, but not part of it, because it is the creating and governing element. As Derrida says, the center is the part of the structure which 'escapes structurality.' In the Puritan example, God creates the world and rules it, and is responsible for it, but isn't part of it. The center is thus, paradoxically, both within the structure and outside it. The center is the center but not part of what Derrida calls 'the totality,' i.e. the structure. So the center is not the center. The concept of the centered structure, according to Derrida, is 'contradictorily coherent.'

In his essay 'Structure, Sign, and Play in the Discourse of the Human Sciences,' originally read at a conference on structuralism at Johns Hopkins University in 1966, Derrida announces that, 'perhaps,' some 'event' or 'rupture' has occurred . The rupture he refers to is what he sees as a major shift in the fundamental structure of Western philosophy. This break is the moment when structuralism enabled philosophy to think about itself differently; with structuralism, it became possible to think about 'the structurality of structure.'

An analogy might be (to paraphrase Plato) to think about being in a room. At first, you think about how to decorate that room: what posters to put up on the walls, where the bed goes, etc. Then one day you might think about your room not as your room, but as one room in a whole building, as part of a structure. Then you might think about the 'roomness' of your room, the qualities that make it a room, and then about how it relates to other rooms in the same building. You might realize that your room is your room, not because of your specific decorations, but because it is not the room next door. The moment when you begin thinking about the roomness of your room is the 'event' Derrida is talking about: the moment when philosophers were able to see their philosophical systems not as absolute truth, but as systems, constructs, structures.

Prior to this rupture or break, according to Derrida, the history of Western philosophy was a continual substitution of one centered system for another centered system, as the rational human mind replaced God, then the unconscious replaced the rational mind, and so on. Structuralism made it possible to see that the center was a construct, not just 'truth,' and to understand the center's function in providing full presence in the system.

Given that Western thought has always utilized a centered system, simply replacing one center for another, Derrida wonders how we can think about, and talk about, systems and centers without creating a new system with a new center. He mentions Nietzsche, Freud, and Heidegger as examples of thinkers who tried to build centerless systems, but failed, and concludes that it is impossible to 'speak outside the system.' In other words, you can't talk about any system of thought without using the terms of that system – there is no 'outside.' Or, in Derrida's words, 'We have no language – no syntax and no lexicon – which is foreign' to a system; 'we can pronounce not a single destructive proposition which has not already had to slip into the form, the logic, and the implicit postulations of precisely what it seeks to contest.'[2]

His example is to think about the concept of 'sign.' As soon as you try to say something like all signs are equal, that there is no transcendental signified that holds a semiotic system together, that signifying systems have no centers, and that therefore all signs have infinite play, or infinite ranges of meaning, you have to note that the only way you can even talk about signs is by using the word 'sign' and assuming that it has some fixed and stable meaning. And then you're back in the system you are trying to 'deconstruct.' This is another reason why Derrida's works, and those of other poststructuralist thinkers, are so difficult to read and understand. They work to write in a way that constantly reminds readers that meaning is unstable, and that makes us aware of the constructed systems which make the text possible.

So what exactly is 'deconstruction,' if Derrida says it's a strategy for reading? What does all this about philosophical systems and centers have to do with reading literature? According to literary theorist Barbara Johnson, deconstruction is 'the careful teasing out of warring forces of signification with the text itself;' a deconstructive reading 'analyzes the specificity of a text's critical difference from itself.'[3] In other words, deconstruction reads a text to see where it posits its own center, how it constructs its own system of 'truth' and 'meaning,' and then looks to see where it contradicts itself. Every text, like every Western philosophical system before Derrida's 'rupture,' creates its own world, with its own terms and premises; like a philosophical system, some idea or concept serves as a center to hold the whole structure together. The basic idea of deconstruction is to find that center and see what happens to the structure if you take it away. The function of the center is to limit play, to hold concepts, such as good and evil, in a firm relation to each other, so that we know what each is, and what side of the slash it should be on. Deconstruction is a way of reading that looks for places where the structure gets shaken up, where more play – more ambiguity of meaning – occurs, where the binary opposites don't stay neatly on their proper side of the slash.

In 'Structure, Sign, and Play' Derrida describes his initial discovery of deconstruction in his reading of Claude Levi-Strauss's *The Elementary Structures of Kinship*. In this book Levi-Strauss says the basic structure of myth, and of all aspects of culture, is the binary pair or opposites, which always have to be the negation of each other. In looking at the dichotomy 'nature/culture,' Levi-Strauss argues that 'nature' is that which is universal and 'culture' is that which is dictated by the norms of a particular social organization. Following the 'grammar' of his structure, then, 'nature' always has to be 'universal' and absolutely opposite of, separate from, 'culture' and 'specific.'

And here Derrida uncovers what he calls 'a scandal,' which illustrates the basic concept of a deconstructive reading. Though Levi-Strauss has set up a system where the terms 'nature' and 'culture' have meaning because they are opposites, one on either side of the slash, his text also discusses the incest prohibition, the law that says who can have sex with whom. The incest prohibition is universal – every culture has one. It is also specific – every culture works out the rules for sex in its own way. Here's something that is *both* universal and specific, both 'nature' and 'culture.' How can that be?

This discovery shakes up Levi-Strauss's system. When two terms refuse to stay on their proper side of the slash, the whole order of the structure gets rattled. A system based on binary opposites depends on all binaries having the same stable structure: good is to evil as light is to dark, as up is to down, as right is to left, as self is to other. If any one of those pairs starts to slide around, to refuse its position in absolute opposition to its partner, then all of the terms start sliding, and pretty soon the formerly stable structure is in pieces. When this happens, you can no longer define one term as the opposite of another – light is what is *not* dark – but when light and dark are no longer opposites, then what do the terms mean? Deconstruction argues that all systems, all texts, have these moments or places where their structures get shaken, and where their formerly solid elements get put into play. Those are the places where a text's definitive meaning breaks down, where multiplicity and ambiguity, rather than clarity and logic, take over. A deconstructive reading thus reads a text against itself, looking for the holes or shaky parts of the system of stable meanings the text tries to set up.

Once you deconstruct a system by pointing out its inconsistencies, by showing what happens when the center fails to hold all the elements in a fixed position, or where the slash dissolves and binaries start to collapse into each other, Derrida says you have two choices. You can throw out the whole structure and try to build another with no inconsistencies, with no play. But of course, according to Derrida, that's impossible; that's just trying to substitute one center for another and not seeing that the center, the transcendental signified, is just a concept, which has play just like any other, and not a fixed and eternal truth.

## BRICOLAGE

The other option, which is Levi-Strauss's choice, is to keep using the structure, but to recognize that it is unstable, that the terms it sets up won't always stay neatly in their designated places, but will have play. In Derrida's terms, this means that the system can no longer claim to be 'true,' but rather that it must acknowledge itself as a construct, as something built around a central idea which was chosen to try to keep everything in place, even though it ultimately cannot keep play away.

Derrida and Levi-Strauss call this method 'bricolage,' and the person who does it a 'bricoleur.' A bricoleur doesn't care about the purity or stability or 'truth' of a system he or she uses, but rather uses what's there to get a particular job done. In philosophical terms, I might want to talk about a belief system and refer to God because that's a useful signifier for something a lot of people believe in; I don't assume that 'God' refers to an actual being, or even to a coherent system of beliefs that situate 'god' at the center and then provides a fixed code of interpretation or behavior. That's why deconstructive readings use a lot of quotation marks; they are a way of indicating that, though you're using a certain signifier as if it had stable meaning, you're aware that it doesn't.

Bricolage doesn't worry about the coherence of the words or ideas it uses. For example, you are a bricoleur if you talk about penis envy or the Oedipus complex without knowing anything about psychoanalysis; you can use the terms without acknowledging the validity or 'truth' of the system that produced these ideas. Bricolage understands meaning not as something eternal and immutable, but as something provisional, something shifting.

Derrida contrasts the bricoleur to the engineer. The engineer designs buildings which have to be solid and have little or no play; the engineer wants to create stable systems or nothing at all. Derrida talks about the engineer as the person who sees himself as the center of his own discourse, the origin of his own language. This guy thinks he speaks language, he originates language, from his own unique existence and experience. The humanist is usually an engineer in this respect.

The idea of bricolage produces a new way to talk about, and think about, systems and structures without falling into the trap of trying to build a new stable system out of the ruins of a deconstructed one. It provides a way to think without establishing a new center, a privileged reference, an origin, a truth. It also inspires creativity and originality, making possible new ways of putting things together.

All systems fall on a continuum between infinite play and eternal stability. Derrida argues that Western culture has always preferred, and desired, systems that seem to be stable, and that promise to always remain the same – to approach what he calls 'full presence,' with no play or fluidity or indeterminacy. Such systems are of course impossible; every system contains its own contradictions and instabilities, which deconstruction can uncover.

The system of language, of which every text is made, has no discernible center – there is no 'God' of language that determines what every word means. As language users, we want language to work both ways. We want language to be a stable structure, so that words have definitive meanings: when I say 'Pass the salt,' I want you to know what I mean without having to interpret my words. And we want language to have lots of play, to be ambiguous, so that we can have multiple meanings for a single word. That's what makes puns and poetry possible. We might want to distinguish between 'everyday' language, where we use words to communicate and hope that those words have a relatively fixed meaning, and 'literary' language, where we use words for their fluidity, because the play of words is pleasurable (as the humanist critics all knew).

## NOTES

1   No, Derrida doesn't take into account tape recordings or virtual realities. Remember, a lot of what these theorists are talking about has roots in philosophical or linguistic traditions that predate most modern technology. Derrida is responding to the opposition speech/writing set up by Plato long before there were tape recorders.
2   Jacques Derrida, 'Structure, Sign, and Play in the Discourse of the Human Sciences,' in Hazard Adams and Leroy Searle, eds, *Critical Theory Since 1965*. Gainesville, FL: University Press of Florida, 1986, p. 85.
3   Barbara Johnson, *The Critical Difference*, cited in *The Penguin Dictionary of Literary Terms and Literary Theory*. New York: Penguin Books, 1998, p. 210.

## SUGGESTIONS FOR FURTHER READING

Jeff Collins, *Introducing Derrida*. New York: Totem Books, 2006.
Jonathan Culler, *On Deconstruction: Theory and Criticism After Structuralism*. Ithaca, NY: Cornell University Press, 1983.
Christopher Norris, *Deconstruction: Theory and Practice*. New York: Routledge, 2002.
James Powell, *Deconstruction for Beginners*. New York: Writers and Readers Publishing Inc., 2005.
Jim Powell and Van Howe, *Derrida for Beginners*. New York: Writers and Readers Publishing Inc., 1996.
Nicholas Royle, *Jacques Derrida*. New York: Routledge, 2003.

# CHAPTER 5

# PSYCHOANALYSIS

## SIGMUND FREUD

Take a moment to think about what you already know about Sigmund Freud and his ideas. He's one of the most important thinkers of the twentieth century, if only because versions of his ideas have permeated almost every aspect of Western culture. It's unlikely that you've never heard of, or used, a Freudian idea – such as a Freudian slip, dream analysis, or even the word 'unconscious.'

Freud was both a medical doctor and a philosopher. As a doctor, he was interested in charting how the human mind affected the body, particularly in forms of mental illness, such as neurosis and hysteria, and in finding ways to cure those mental illnesses. As a philosopher, Freud was interested in looking at the relationship between mental functioning and certain basic structures of civilization, such as incest taboos or religious beliefs. Freud believed, and many people after him believe, that his theories about how the mind worked uncovered some basic universal truths about how an individual self is formed, and how culture and civilization operate.

When Freud looks at 'civilization' (which he does in *Civilization and its Discontents*), he sees two fundamental principles at work, which he calls the 'pleasure principle' and the 'reality principle.' The pleasure principle tells us to do whatever feels good; the reality principle tells us to subordinate pleasure to what needs to be done, to work. Subordinating the pleasure principle to the reality principle is done through a psychological process Freud calls *sublimation*, where you take desires that can't be fulfilled, or shouldn't be fulfilled, and turn their energy into something useful and productive. A typical Freudian example of this would focus on sex. Sex is pleasurable; for Freud, sexual pleasure is the model for all forms of pleasure. The desire for sexual pleasure, according to Freud, is one of the oldest and most basic urges all humans feel; the desire for sexual pleasure begins pretty much with birth. But humans can't just have sex all the time. If we did, we'd never get any work done. So we have to sublimate most of our desires for sexual pleasure, and turn that sexual energy into something else – into writing a paper, for example, or playing sports. Freud says that, without the sublimation of our sexual desires into more productive realms, there would be no civilization.

The pleasure principle makes us want to do things that feel good, while the reality principle tells us to channel that energy elsewhere. But the desire for pleasure doesn't disappear, even when it's sublimated into work. The desires that can't be fulfilled are packed, or *repressed*, into a particular place in the mind, which Freud labels the *unconscious*.

Because it contains repressed desires, things that our conscious mind isn't supposed to want, and isn't supposed to know about, the unconscious is by definition inaccessible to the conscious mind. You can't know what's in your unconscious by thinking about it directly. However, there are some indirect routes into the contents of the unconscious.

The first, and perhaps the most familiar, is dreams. According to Freud in *The Interpretation of Dreams*, dreams are symbolic fulfillments of wishes that can't be fulfilled because they've been repressed. Often these wishes can't even be expressed directly in consciousness, because they are forbidden, so they come out in dreams – but in strange ways, in ways that often hide or disguise the true (forbidden) wish behind the dream.

Dreams use two main mechanisms to disguise forbidden wishes: *condensation* and *displacement*. Condensation is when a whole set of images is packed into a single image or statement, when a complex meaning is condensed into a simpler one. Condensation corresponds to *metaphor* in language, where one thing is condensed into another. 'Love is a rose, and you'd better not pick it:' this metaphor condenses all the qualities of love, including its sweetness and its pain, into a single image. Displacement is where the meaning of one image or symbol gets pushed onto something associated with it, which then displaces the original image. Displacement corresponds to the mechanism of *metonymy* in language, where one thing is replaced by something corresponding to it or associated with it. An example of metonymy is when you evoke an image of a whole thing by naming a part of it – when you say 'the crown' when you mean 'the queen' or 'royalty,' or you say 'twenty sails' when you mean 'twenty ships.' You displace the idea of the whole thing onto a part associated with it. You might think of condensation and metaphor as being like Saussure's syntagmatic relations, which happen in a chain and displacement and metonymy being like Saussure's associative relations.

Another way into the unconscious besides dreams is what Freud calls *parapraxes*, or slips of the tongue; he discusses these in *The Psychopathology of Everyday Life*. Such mistakes, including errors in speech, reading, and writing, are not coincidences or accidents, Freud says. Rather, they reveal something that has been repressed into the unconscious. A third way into the unconscious is jokes, which Freud says are always indicative of repressed wishes. He discusses this route into the unconscious in *Jokes and Their Relation to the Unconscious*.

You can probably tell from these three routes into the unconscious – dreams, parapraxes, and jokes – that psychoanalysis asks us to pay a lot of attention to language, in puns, slips of the tongue, displacements and condensations, etc. This suggests how psychoanalysis is directly related to literary criticism, since both kinds of analysis focus on close readings of language.

Whatever route is taken into the unconscious, what you find there, according to Freud, is almost always about sex. The contents of the unconscious consist primarily of sexual desires which have been repressed. Freud says that sexual desires are instinctual and that they appear in the most fundamental acts in the process of nurturing, like in a mother nursing an infant. The instincts for food, warmth, and comfort, which have survival value for an infant, also produce pleasure, which Freud defines specifically as sexual pleasure. He says our first experiences of our bodies are organized through how we experience sexual pleasure; he divides the infant's experience of its body into certain *erotogenic zones*. The first erotogenic zone is the mouth, as the baby feels sexual pleasure in its mouth while nursing. Because the act of sucking is pleasurable (and, for Freud, all pleasure is sexual pleasure), the baby forms a bond with its mother that goes beyond the satisfaction of the baby's hunger. That bond Freud calls *libidinal*, since it involves the baby's *libido*, the drive for sexual pleasure.

These erotogenic zones are the *oral*, the *anal*, and the *phallic*, and they correspond to three major stages of childhood development. They take place roughly between the ages of 2 and 5, though Freud was often revising his estimate of the ages when these stages occurred; later psychoanalysts argue that the oral stage begins soon after birth, with the first experience of nursing, and that the phallic stage ends somewhere between ages 3 and 5. The exact ages at which an infant goes through these stages are less important in understanding psychoanalysis as a theory, than understanding what those stages represent. The oral stage is associated with incorporation, with taking things in, with knowing no boundaries between self and other, inside and outside. The anal stage (which Freud says has a lot to do with toilet training) is associated with expelling things, with learning boundaries between inside and outside, and with aggression and anger. The phallic stage – and Freud argues that 'phallic' refers to both penis and clitoris, and is common to both boys and girls – leads a child toward genital masturbation, and hence to the gateway of adult sexuality.

It's important to note that the child Freud is describing in his *Three Essays on the Theory of Sexuality* and other writings is *polymorphously perverse*, a term Freud uses to describe a being whose sexual or libidinal drives are relatively unorganized, and are directed at any and every object that might provide sexual pleasure. The child experiences an erotic, or erotogenic, pleasure any time one of these erotogenic zones – oral, anal, and phallic – is stimulated; these pleasures persist into adult life.

The polymorphously perverse child is pleasure-seeking. It is not yet under the sway of the reality principle, and because it doesn't have to repress any of its desires, it has no unconscious. Without an unconscious, or the repression that creates it, or the reality principle that demands repression (which is associated with what Freud calls the *superego*), the child has no gender. Freud does, however, define all libidinal drives as masculine.

Because the desiring child will go after anything that might provide pleasure, and because its first experiences of pleasure have come through its contact with its mother, the child is *incestuous*, desiring the pleasure that comes from contact with its mother's body. The mother's body becomes pleasurable through oral contact, in nursing, through cuddling and being held, through the mother making the child aware of its anal region, in diaper changing and toilet training, and through the mother making the child aware of the pleasure in its genitals, usually through cleaning and bathing.

Polymorphous perversity is the earliest stage of child sexual development, according to Freud; it may last till age 5 or 6. Then the child enters the *latency* period, where the instinctual drives and libidinal explorations of the polymorphously perverse phase are put on hold; the child doesn't think about, or go after, sexual pleasure (at least not so directly and constantly) any more. The search for sexual pleasure is revived at puberty, the third – and final – stage in sexual development, for Freud. At puberty, the instinctual urges from infancy take on 'adult' characteristics, and get directed toward 'normal' aims. At puberty, sexual drives turn from being *autoerotic* (that is, masturbatory, or directed at one's own body as a source of pleasure) to being directed at an *object*, another person. These sexual desires also acquire a new *aim*, which is not just pleasurable stimulation but orgasm. If all works well, at puberty all of the polymorphously perverse drives of infancy get channeled into reproductive heterosexual intercourse, and all the erotic feelings generated in the erotogenic zones get subordinated to the genital zone alone. The old erotogenic zones become places to provide forepleasure, which leads up to reproductive heterosexual intercourse, which Freud defines as the only normal adult form of sexual pleasure.

The project of psychoanalysis in general is to chart how this polymorphously perverse incestuous desiring animal turns into a self with a firm sense of differentiated gender (masculine or feminine), with sexual and libidinal desires channeled into proper forms (defined as non-incestuous reproductive heterosexuality), and subordinated to the reality principle so that this self can get some work done and not just have sex all the time. The project of psychoanalytic *theory* is to describe how the gendered and sexual self is formed. The project of Freud's psychoanalytic *practice* (and many of those who followed him) was to cure those who had gone astray in the process, those who had not correctly developed this firm sense of gender, sexuality, and repression of libidinal drives.

It is worth noting, however, that Freud wasn't particularly interested in curing what he called 'perversions,' or sexual behaviors that don't fit into the non-incestuous reproductive heterosexual model. In *Three Essays on the Theory of Sexuality* Freud discusses perversions as libidinal drives that may be socially inappropriate (or even illegal), but which get expressed and acted on; neuroses, by contrast, are libidinal drives that get repressed into the unconscious, but which are so powerful that the unconscious has to spend a lot of energy to keep these drives from coming back into consciousness. The effort required to keep such ideas or drives repressed can cause hysteria, paranoia, obsession-compulsion, and other neurotic disorders.

The main vehicle for the construction of properly gendered and sexual selves is the *Oedipus Complex*. The Oedipus Complex is what ends the phallic phase, and the polymorphous perverse phase in general, and forces the child into the latency phase. Freud hints at the foundations of the Oedipus Complex when he talks about castration and penis envy, and about the infantile idea that both males and females have penises.

As Freud describes it, going through the Oedipus Complex as a developmental stage in childhood turns us from incestuous sexual desire to exogamous (outside the family) sexual desire, hence from a state of nature to one of culture or civilization. The Oedipus Complex explains how desires get repressed, how these repressed desires form the unconscious, how girls and boys learn to desire objects outside of their own families, how each sex learns to desire someone of the opposite sex, and how the superego – the reality principle, or what we call 'conscience' – gets formed.

To understand the operations of the Oedipus Complex, we have to look at what Freud says is 'The Differentiation Between Men and Women,' the title of the third of his *Three Essays on the Theory of Sexuality*. Here Freud defines what is 'masculine' as what is active; what is passive is likewise defined as 'feminine.' Both sexes are 'masculine' in regards to infantile sexuality, which is active in seeking pleasure, especially through masturbation.

> So far as the autoerotic and masturbatory manifestations of sexuality are concerned, we might lay it down that the sexuality of little girls is of a wholly masculine character. Indeed, if we were able to give a more definite connotation to the concepts of 'masculine' and 'feminine,' it would even be possible to maintain that libido is invariably and necessarily of a masculine nature, whether it occurs in men or in women, and irrespective of whether its object is a man or a woman.[1]

According to Freud, the masculine part of the girl is the clitoris, which corresponds to the penis in boys; in fact, Freud calls the clitoris a miniature penis. With puberty, girls experience a great wave of repression of clitoridal sexuality (masturbation), accompanied by feelings of disgust and shame at the idea of masturbation, and sex in general. This repression of what Freud calls a 'masculine' sexuality is necessary for girls to become feminine, i.e. passive. Boys, meanwhile, at puberty experience a great increase in masculine libido, rather than a repression of it. Freud also says that the more girls repress their clitoral feelings, the more excited boys get, as they desire more and more the girls who offer less and less sexual access. In adult sexuality, clitoridal stimulation is part of forepleasure, leading to correct vaginal stimulation via reproductive heterosexual intercourse. As an end in itself, clitoridal stimulation is considered infantile and neurotic in Freudian theory.

Thus the girl, or woman, at puberty has the task of switching primary erotogenic zones, from the clitoris which was the focus of her pleasure in the phallic stage to the vagina, which is to become the focus of her pleasure in adult reproductive heterosexual intercourse in order to become a 'normal' adult. The boy, or man, meanwhile gets to stick with his phallic zone and focus his adult sexuality, like his infantile sexuality, on the pleasure he gets from his penis.

> The fact that women change their leading erotogenic zone in this way, together with the wave of repression in puberty, which, as it were, puts aside their childish masculinity, are the chief determinants of the greater proneness of women to neurosis and especially to hysteria. These determinants, therefore, are intimately related to the essence of femininity.[2]

In addition to having to shift erotogenic zones in order to reach the proper adult form of sexuality, Freud says, women also have to shift objects. Both the boy and the girl take their mother as their first love object, because their experience of the mother's body is associated for them with the first experiences of pleasure. In the transformation from polymorphously perverse infant to sexually proper adult, the boy keeps the female body as his love-object – he just switches from his mother's body to the bodies of other women, those unrelated to him. The girl, however, whose primary erotic attachment was also to the mother's body, has to shift her erotic feelings to a male body in order to achieve normal adult non-incestuous heterosexuality. This double-shifting required of the girl – from clitoris to vagina and from a female body as erotic object to a male body – creates the potential for a lot of neurosis. And that's part of Freud's overall view of femininity: women, that is, 'proper' women who are oriented solely toward non-incestuous reproductive adult heterosexuality, are pretty neurotic.

The way that girls and boys make these shifts in erotogenic zones and erotic objects is through the Oedipus Complex, which Freud explains in detail in 'Some Psychological Consequences of the Anatomical Distinction Between the Sexes' (1925). At some point when the infant is negotiating the three erotogenic zones, usually in the phallic phase (a phase shared by boys and girls, since the clitoris is phallic), children notice the anatomical distinction between the sexes, or in Freud's terms, that boys have penises and girls do not. Prior to this, according to Freud, each sex thought the other had the same equipment it did.

The boy's reaction to seeing the girl's lack of penis is first to disavow this new knowledge, and insist that she has one. Eventually, however, he comes to realize that the girl hasn't got a penis; he sees this as lack or absence, and decides her penis has been cut off as punishment for some transgression.

At this point, in the phallic phase, the boy has discovered phallic masturbation and, according to Freud, he wants to direct this phallic activity toward his mother, whom he desires or loves, with 'libidinal cathexis.' Because of this sexual love for his mother, the boy wants to get rid of his father as his rival for his mother's love – more specifically, he wants to kill his father so he can 'marry,' i.e. have sole sexual possession of, his mother. This is the Oedipus Complex in boys: the desire to kill the father so that he can fulfill his libidinal desire for his mother.

Having developed these feelings of sexual desire for his mother and anger and aggression towards his father, the boy perceives the 'fact' of the girl's castration and develops *castration anxiety* – the fear that his father, angry at the boy's desire to kill him and have sex with the father's woman, will cut off his penis in revenge. The boy then enters into the *castration complex*, which forces him to choose between wanting his mother and losing his penis. Fearing the anger of the father, and the loss of his penis, the boy gives up his desire for his mother, thus ending the Oedipus Complex and creating the unconscious, which is the place where all his unfillable and inexpressible desires – starting with his desire for his mother – will go.

The desire for the mother goes into and creates the unconscious. The fear of the father creates the *superego*, which will be the place where the voices of authority and conscience reside. All subsequent prohibitions on behavior, whether from parents, teachers, laws, police, religious authorities, or whatever, will join this initial prohibition in the superego, and will shape the boy's sense of morality, of right and wrong. Hence the abandonment of incestuous desire, under the threat of castration, forms the basis of instilling and enforcing the reality principle and subduing the pleasure principle. At the instigation of the superego, inexpressible and impermissible desires and pleasures will be repressed into the unconscious, and emerge in other forms – as sublimations, neuroses, 'reaction formations,' and in dreams, slips of the tongue, and jokes. Freud thus charts the human mind as containing three basic areas or functions, all of which emerge as a result of the resolution of the Oedipus Complex by the castration complex: the unconscious, the superego, and the consciousness, or sense of self.

After this, the path is pretty clear for the boy. He identifies with his father, and with his father's authority to prohibit incestuous desire. He understands that, if he's good, he'll get a woman of his own someday, and, with his own children, wield the authority his father has. Thus all he has to do is wait to fulfill his libidinal urges in the proper non-incestuous reproductive heterosexual way.

For the girl, this trajectory is much more complicated and involves a lot of double-shifting, as we've noted: from clitoris to vagina, from mother's body to a male body. Freud ties himself up in knots trying to explain how girls do this. The difficulties Freud had in explaining the female route to adult non-incestuous reproductive heterosexuality should have told him that his model, based on what boys experience, was flawed – but it didn't. Psychoanalysis as both theory and method has suffered ever since from these sexist roots.

First of all, the girl notices that boys have penises and girls don't. Freud says the girl instantly recognizes the penis as the superior counterpart to the clitoris, and falls victim to *penis envy*: 'She has seen it and knows that she is without it and wants to have it.'[3]

From that point, the girl can go in a couple of directions. She can deny that she has no penis, and persist in thinking that she does, which can lead to psychosis. She may fixate on the idea of someday getting a penis, by whatever means possible. Or she can take the 'normal' route, which is to accept 'the fact of her castration.' If she accepts this 'fact,' she develops a sense of inferiority to the male; she decides her lack of a penis is the punishment for some wrongdoing (probably masturbation); she gets furious with her mother for not giving her a penis, and for not having one herself; she feels contempt for the entire female sex, herself included, which is without such an important organ. Also, she feels the clitoris to be so inferior that she gives up masturbation entirely. Freud says clitoral masturbation is entirely masculine and the girl's recognition of her lack of a penis makes her repudiate all her masculine activities, and to feel a great disgust at the idea of masturbation.

An important consequence of her penis envy, and acceptance of the 'fact' of her castration, aside from just the internalized sense of female inferiority Freud insists on, is the loosening of her bond with her mother. On discovering that her mother doesn't have a penis, and didn't give her one, the girl takes the libidinal desire she, like the boy, felt for the mother and turns it into anger and hatred for not giving her a penis. This moves her toward the necessary shift to taking her father as libidinal object.

The girl then decides that, if she can't have a penis, she'll have a baby instead, and takes her father as her erotic object with the express purpose of having her father's baby; her mother in turn becomes solely an object of jealousy and rivalry.

At this point, Freud announces, 'The girl has turned into a little woman.'[4] This is the Oedipus Complex for girls, which Freud first called the 'Electra Complex,' but in later works called the feminine or negative Oedipus Complex. It starts when the girl begins to desire her father and hate her mother.

Hence in girls the castration complex comes first – they realize they *are* castrated, then they enter into an oedipal relation, desiring to kill the mother and marry the father and have his baby. For boys, remember, it was the other way around: the castration complex ends the Oedipus Complex. With the girl, castration has already been carried out – there's nothing to lose – whereas with the boy it is only threatened.

If for boys the castration complex ends the Oedipus Complex, and creates the unconscious and the superego, and pushes the boy into adult non-incestuous reproductive heterosexual sexuality, what happens with girls?

Freud is at best fuzzy on this. He says that the oedipal feelings in girls may be repressed, but he doesn't say how, or that it may be abandoned, though he doesn't say how, or that it may just fade away (ditto), or that it may persist. The result is that women never really do form a strong superego because they don't have a strong motive to repress forbidden desires and to form a place where the voice of authority will dwell. The worst has already happened, girls have lost their penises, so what is there to be afraid of? The consequence of having a weaker or less formed superego, according to Freud, is that women are not as moral or just as men; women go by their feelings and not their sense of reason and justice. Freud is also not quite sure how women form an unconscious, since they don't have castration anxiety as the motive to repress their incestuous wishes; some sort of repression happens, but Freud isn't entirely clear on how or what. This means that a woman's unconscious may be less well anchored than a man's, that a woman's unconscious wishes are less firmly repressed, and more likely to rise up into consciousness. For Freud, the weakness of the female superego and unconscious explain why women are not suitable to be the rulers and shapers of civilization.

Freud tries, in subsequent essays such as 'Female Sexuality,' (1931) and 'Femininity' (1933), to explain further the female movement through the Oedipus Complex. He never gets very far. He ends up saying that women stay in the Oedipus Complex for ever, since nothing ends it for them, and that they always pretty much desire their fathers. Somehow they learn to become non-incestuous, but they usually end up marrying men who are like their fathers. Feminist critics, as you may imagine, have a lot to say about Freud's ideas of gender. To Freud, women were never fully comprehensible: he referred to women, finally, as 'the dark continent.'[5]

## JACQUES LACAN

In his discussion of the absolute division between the unconscious and the consciousness, between id and ego, Freud introduces the idea of the human self, or subject, as radically split, divided between the two realms of consciousness and unconsciousness. For Freud, and for psychoanalysis in general, actions, thoughts, belief, and the idea of the 'self' are all primarily determined by the unconscious and its drives and desires.

Jacques Lacan was a French psychoanalyst. He was originally trained as a psychiatrist, and in the 1930s and 1940s worked with psychotic patients. He began in the 1950s to develop his own version of psychoanalysis, based on the ideas being articulated in structuralist linguistics and anthropology. You might think of Lacan as Freud plus Saussure, with a dash of Levi-Strauss and even some seasoning of Derrida. But his main influence and precursor is Freud. Lacan reinterprets Freud in light of structuralist and poststructuralist theories, turning psychoanalysis from an essentially humanist philosophy or theory into a poststructuralist one.

One of the basic premises of humanism, as you will recall, is that there is such a thing as a stable self, that has all those nice things like free will and self-determination. Freud's notion of the unconscious was one of the ideas that began to question, or to destabilize and deconstruct, that humanist ideal of the self; Freud's ideas took the rational mind out of the center of the humanist philosophical system, but replaced it with the unconscious as the center of his psychoanalytic system. But Freud still hoped for a return to the humanist model that placed consciousness and rationality at the center; he hoped that, by bringing the contents of the unconscious into consciousness, he could minimize repression and neurosis. Freud makes a famous declaration about the ideal relation between unconscious and consciousness, predicting that, through psychoanalysis, 'Wo Es war, soll Ich werden:' 'Where It was, shall I be.'[6] In other words, the 'it' or 'id,' the unconscious, will be replaced by the 'I,' by consciousness and self-identity. Freud's goal was to strengthen the ego, the 'I' self, the conscious rational identity, so it would be ultimately more powerful than, and able to control, the unconscious.

For Lacan, this project is impossible. The ego can never take the place of the unconscious, or empty it out, or control it, because for Lacan the ego or 'I' self is only an illusion, a product of the unconscious itself. In Lacanian psychoanalysis, the unconscious is the ground of all being.

Where Freud is interested in investigating how the polymorphously perverse child forms an unconscious and a superego and becomes a civilized (i.e. materially productive and correctly heterosexual) adult, Lacan is interested in how the infant gets this illusion that Western humanist thought has called a 'self.' In 'The Mirror Stage as Formative of the Function of the I as Revealed in Psychoanalytic Experience' (1949), Lacan describes that process, showing how the infant forms an illusion of an ego, of a unified conscious self identified by the signifier 'I.'

Central to the conception of the human, in Lacan, is the notion that the unconscious, which governs all factors of human existence, is structured like a language. He bases this on Freud's account of the two main mechanisms of unconscious processes, condensation and displacement. Both are essentially linguistic phenomena, where meaning is either condensed, as in metaphor, or displaced, as in metonymy. Lacan notes that Freud's dream analysis, and most of his analyses of the unconscious symbolism used by his patients, depends on word-play: on puns, associations, etc., that are chiefly verbal. Lacan says that the contents of the unconscious are acutely aware of language, and particularly of the structure of language.

When Lacan talks about the structure of language, he follows the ideas laid out by Saussure, but modifies them a bit. Where Saussure talked about the relations between signifier and signified, which form a sign, and insisted that the structure of language is the negative relation of value among signs (one sign is what it is because it is not another sign), Lacan focuses on relations between signifiers alone. The elements in the unconscious – wishes, desires, images – are all signifiers, and they are usually expressed in verbal terms. These signifiers form a 'signifying chain:' one signifier has meaning only because it is not some other signifier. For Lacan, there are no signifieds; there is nothing a signifier ultimately refers to. If there were, then the meaning of any particular signifier would be relatively stable: there would be a relation of signification between signifier and signified, and that relation would guarantee some kind of fixed meaning. Lacan says that relations of signification don't exist in the unconscious; rather, there are only negative relations, relations of value, where one signifier has meaning only in relation to all the signifiers it's not.

Because of this lack of signifieds, Lacan says, the chain of signifiers – $x=y=f=h=e=q=\%=\&=?=\#=s=k=c$ – is constantly sliding and shifting and circulating. There is no anchor, no center, nothing that ultimately gives meaning or stability to any single signifier or to the whole chain of signifiers. The chain of signifiers is constantly in play, in Derrida's sense; there's no way to stop sliding from one signifier to the next, to say, 'Oh, x means this,' and have it be definitive. Rather, one signifier leads to another signifier leads to another signifier, and never to a signified or an end. It's like a dictionary: when you look up the meaning of a word, you get more words (which you can then look up, and get more words) but you never get to the thing the word supposedly represents.

Lacan says the unconscious looks like a continually circulating chain, or multiply linked chains, of signifiers, with no anchor, with no (Derridean) center. This is Lacan's linguistic translation of Freud's picture of the unconscious as a chaotic realm of constantly shifting drives and desires. Freud is interested in how to bring those chaotic drives and desires into consciousness, so that they can have some order and sense and meaning, so they can be understood and made manageable. Lacan, on the other hand, says that the process of becoming an adult, a 'self,' is the process of trying to fix, to stabilize, to stop the circulation of the chain of signifiers so that stable meaning – including, and represented by, the meaning of the word 'I' – becomes possible. Though Lacan of course says that this possibility is only an illusion, an image created by a misperception of the relation between body and self.

Notice what a peculiar kind of signifier 'I' is, even within a stable system like Saussure's. 'I' has value, like all other signifiers in the system of English, because it's not any of the other signifiers in English. For Saussure, though, 'I' would also have signification because the signifier 'I' is linked to a concept, the signified, which is identity or selfhood of an individual. But the signified for 'I' shifts every time someone uses it: when I say 'I,' I mean me (Mary, professor, author) – but if you say 'I,' you mean yourself, not me. The signifier is the same in both cases – 'I' – but the signified changes according to the speaker using it. This doesn't happen, supposedly, with most signifiers: if I say 'page 102' and you say 'page 102,' we assume we're referring to the same signified, page 102.

### The Real, the Imaginary, and the Symbolic

Freud talks about the three stages of polymorphous perversity in infants: the oral, anal, and phallic stages. The Oedipus Complex, leading to the Castration Complex, end polymorphous perversity and create 'adult' beings (at least for boys). Lacan creates different categories to explain a similar trajectory from infant to 'adult.' He talks about three concepts – need, demand, and desire – that roughly correspond to three phases of development, or three fields in which humans develop – the Real, the Imaginary, and the Symbolic. The Symbolic realm, which is marked by the concept of desire, is the equivalent of adulthood. More specifically, for Lacan the Symbolic realm is the structure of language itself, which we have to enter into in order to become speaking subjects, in order to say 'I' and 'page 102' and have them both designate something which appears to be stable.

Like Freud's, Lacan's infant starts out as something inseparable from its mother; there's no distinction between self and other, between baby and mother (at least, from the baby's perspective). In fact, the baby, for both Freud and Lacan, is a kind of blob, with no sense of self or individuated identity, and no sense even of its body as a coherent unified whole. This baby-blob is driven by need: it needs food, it needs comfort, it needs safety, it needs to be changed, etc. These needs are satisfiable, and can be satisfied by an object. When the baby needs food, it gets a breast (or a bottle); when it needs safety, it gets hugged. The baby, in this state of need, doesn't recognize any distinction between itself and the objects that meet its needs; it doesn't recognize that an object, like a breast, is part of another whole person, because it doesn't yet have any concept of 'whole person.' There's no distinction between it and anyone or anything else; there are only needs and things that satisfy those needs.

This is a state of 'nature,' which has to be broken up in order for culture to be formed. This is true in both Freud's psychoanalysis and in Lacan's: the infant must separate from its mother, form a separate identity, in order to enter into civilization. That separation entails some kind of *loss*. When the child knows the difference between itself and its mother, and starts to become an individuated being, it loses that primal sense of unity (and of safety/security) it originally had. This is the element of the tragic built into psychoanalytic theory, whether Freudian or Lacanian: to become a civilized adult always entails the profound loss of an original unity, a non-differentiation, an unselfhood.

The baby who has not yet made this separation, who has only needs which are satisfiable, and which makes no distinction between itself and the objects that satisfy its needs, exists in the realm of the Real, according to Lacan. The Real is a (psychic) place where there is this original unity. Because of that, there is no absence or loss or lack; the Real is all fullness and completeness, where there's no need that can't be satisfied. And because there is no absence or loss or lack, there is no language in the Real.

Lacan here follows an argument Freud made about the idea of loss. In his essay *Beyond the Pleasure Principle*, Freud talks about his nephew, aged about 18 months, who is playing a game with a spool tied with yarn. The kid throws the spool away and says 'fort,' which is German for 'gone.' He pulls the spool back in, and says 'da,' which is German for 'here.' Freud says that this game was symbolic for the kid, a way of working out his anxiety about his mother's absence. When he threw the spool away and said 'fort,' he replayed the experience of the loss of a beloved object; when he reeled it in and said 'da,' he got pleasure from the restoration of the object, and from his mastery of the anxiety-producing situation.

Lacan takes this case and focuses, of course, on the aspect of language it displays. Lacan says that the fort/da game concerns the child's entry into the Symbolic, or into the structure of language itself. Lacan says that language is always about loss or absence: you only need words when the object you want isn't present. If your world was all fullness, with no absence or emptiness, then you wouldn't need language.

Thus, in the realm of the Real, according to Lacan, there is no language because there is no loss, no lack, no absence; there is only complete fullness, only needs and the satisfaction of needs. Hence the Real is always beyond language, unrepresentable in language, and therefore irretrievably lost when one enters into language.

The Real, and the phase of need, lasts from birth till somewhere between 6 and 18 months, when the baby-blob starts to be able to distinguish between its body and everything else in the world. At this point the baby shifts from having needs to having demands. Demands are not satisfiable with objects; a demand is always a demand for recognition from another, for love from another. The process works like this: the baby starts to become aware that it is separate from the mother, that there are times when the mother is gone; it also begins to become aware that there exist things that are not part of it. This is how the idea of 'other' is created. Note, however, that as yet the binary opposition of self/other doesn't yet exist, because the baby doesn't have any coherent sense of self. The awareness of separation, of the possibility of 'other,' creates an anxiety, a sense of loss. The baby then demands a reunion, a return to the original state of fullness and non-separation that it had in the Real. But that's impossible, once the baby knows (and remember, all this 'knowing' happens unconsciously) that the concept of 'other' exists. The baby demands to be filled by the other, to return to the original sense of unity; the baby wants the idea of 'other' to disappear. Demand is thus the demand for the fullness, the completeness, of the other that will stop up the lack the baby is experiencing. But of course this is impossible, because that lack, or absence, the sense of 'other'ness, is the condition for the baby becoming a self, a subject in language, a functioning cultural being.

Because the demand is for recognition from the other, it can't really be satisfied, if only because a 6- to 18-month-old can't say what it wants. The baby cries, and the mother gives it a breast or bottle, or a pacifier, or something, but no object can satisfy the demand. The demand is for a response on a different level. The baby can't recognize the ways its care-giver does respond to it, and recognize it, because it doesn't yet have a conception of itself as a thing. The infant knows only that 'other' exists, and that 'other' means separation; it doesn't yet know what 'self' is.

This is where Lacan's *mirror stage* happens. At this age the baby hasn't yet mastered its own body; it doesn't have control over its own movements, and it doesn't have a sense of its body as a connected whole – the baby is only beginning to realize that the thumb that occasionally drifts by its mouth, and which it sucks, is its own thumb. Mostly the baby experiences its body as fragmented, or in pieces. However, the baby at this stage can imagine itself as whole, because it has seen other people, and perceived them as whole beings. This perception comes through vision: when the baby looks at another person, it sees all of him or her in one moment, in one complete experience. Vision gives us the perception of whole pictures, unlike touch, which has to comprehend an object by feeling all its parts and trying to piece those sensations together.

Lacan says that, at some point during this period, the baby will see itself in a mirror. It will look at its reflection, then look back at a real person – its mother, or some other person, then look again at the mirror image. Usually the other person is there saying to the baby, 'Yes, look, it's you! It's baby! Do you see baby?' The baby moves 'from insufficiency to anticipation' in this action: the mirror, the looking back and forth between a real person and the mirror image, and the person who reinforces all this by saying 'It's you!' all give the baby the sense that it too is an integrated whole. Prior to this the baby knew that others were whole, since it had perceived them visually in the instantaneous wholeness vision provides; it also knew that others were separate from it. In the mirror stage, the baby begins to anticipate being whole. It moves from a 'fragmented body' to an 'orthopedic vision of its totality,' to a vision of itself as whole and integrated, just like others; the vision is 'orthopedic' because it serves as a crutch, a corrective and supportive instrument, which will help the child imagine itself as whole.

What the child anticipates is a sense of 'self,' a sense of identity as a unified and separate whole being. The child begins to understand that what it sees in the mirror looks like what it sees when it looks at other real people. The verbal reinforcment – 'It's you!' – helps the baby learn that the entity in the mirror, which the baby sees as whole, is the signified designated by the words 'you' or 'I' – the baby begins to see that the entity in the mirror is its 'self.'

What is really happening, however, is an identification that is a *misrecognition*, or what Lacan calls *méconnaissance*. The child sees an image in the mirror. It thinks, 'That's ME!' But it's not the child – it's only an image the child sees. The other person is there to reinforce the misrecognition with that shifting pronoun 'you' – 'Yes! It's YOU!' The other person gives the linguistic name, the signifier, that will go with the image the baby sees, and guarantees the 'reality' of the connection between the child and its image, between the signifier 'I' (or 'you') and the image, and between the picture of the whole body in the mirror and the child's sense of itself as a whole integrated being.

The child takes that image in the mirror as the summation of its entire being, its 'self.' This process of misrecognizing one's self in the image in the mirror creates the ego, the entity that says 'I.' In Lacan's terms, this misrecognition creates the 'armor' of the subject, an illusion or misperception of wholeness, integration, and totality that surrounds and protects the fragmented body. To Lacan, ego, or self, or 'I'dentity, is always on some level a fantasy, an identification with an external image, and not an internal sense of separate wholeness.

This is why Lacan calls the phase of demand, and the mirror stage, the realm of the Imaginary. The idea of a self is created through an Imaginary identification with the image in the mirror. The realm of the Imaginary is where the alienated relation of self to its own image is created and maintained. The Imaginary is a realm of images, whether conscious or unconscious. It's prelinguistic and pre-oedipal, but very much based in visual perception, or what Lacan calls specular imaging.

The mirror image, the whole person the baby mistakes as itself, is known in psychoanalytic terminology as an 'ideal ego,' a perfect whole self who has no insufficiency. This 'ideal ego' becomes internalized; we build our sense of 'self,' our 'I'dentity, by (mis)identifying with this ideal ego. By doing this, according to Lacan, we imagine a self that has no lack, no notion of absence or incompleteness. The fiction of the stable, whole unified self that we see in the mirror becomes a compensation for having lost the original oneness with the mother's body. In short, according to Lacan, we lose our unity with the mother's body, the state of 'nature' in the realm of the Real, in order to enter culture and language, but we protect ourselves from the knowledge of that loss by misperceiving ourselves as not lacking anything – as being complete unto ourselves.

Lacan says that the child's self-concept (its ego or 'I'dentity) will never match up to its own being. Its *imago* in the mirror is both smaller and more stable than the child, and is always 'other' than the child – something outside it. The child, for the rest of its life, will misrecognize its self as 'other,' as the image in the mirror that provides an illusion of self and of mastery.

The Imaginary is the psychic place, or phase, where the child projects its ideas of 'self' onto the mirror image it sees. The mirror stage cements a self/other dichotomy, where previously the child had known 'other' but not 'self.' For Lacan, the identification of 'self' is always in terms of 'other.' This is not the same as the binary opposition where 'self' is defined as 'what is not other' and 'other' is defined as 'what is not self.' Rather, 'self' *is* 'other,' in Lacan's view; the idea of the self, that inner being we designate by 'I,' is based on an image, an other. The concept of self relies on one's misidentification with the image of an other.

Lacan uses the term 'other' in a number of ways, which makes it even more difficult to grasp. First, and perhaps easiest, is the sense of self/other, where 'other' is the 'not-me;' but as we have seen, the 'other' becomes 'me' in the mirror stage. Lacan also uses an idea of Other, with a capital 'O,' to distinguish between the concept of the other and actual others. The image the child sees in the mirror is an other, and gives the child the idea of Other as a structural possibility, one which makes possible the structural possibility of 'I' or self. In other words, the child encounters actual others – other people, its own image – and understands the idea of 'Otherness,' things that are not itself. According to Lacan, the notion of Otherness, encountered in the Imaginary phase (and associated with demand) comes before the sense of 'self,' which is built on the idea of Otherness.

When the child has formulated some idea of Otherness, and of a self identified with its own 'other,' its own mirror image, then the child begins to enter the Symbolic realm. The Symbolic and the Imaginary are overlapping, unlike Freud's phases of development; there's no clear marker or division between the two, and in some respects they always co-exist, the Symbolic like an overlay blanketing the Imaginary. The Symbolic order is the structure of language itself. We have to enter this structure in order to become speaking subjects, to use signifiers as if they were connected to signifieds, as if words made meaning, and especially to designate our self by saying 'I.' The foundation for having a self lies in the Imaginary projection of the self onto the specular image, the other in the mirror, and having a self is expressed in saying 'I,' which can only occur within the Symbolic, which is why the two co-exist.

The fort/da game Freud describes is in Lacan's view a marker of the entry into the Symbolic, because Freud's Yaung nephew is using language to negotiate the idea of absence and the idea of Otherness as a category or structural possibility. The spool, for Lacan, serves as an *objet petit a,'* or *'objet petit autre'* – an object which is a little 'other,' a small-'o' other. In throwing the spool away, the child recognizes that others can disappear; in pulling it back, the child recognizes that others can return. Lacan emphasizes the former, insisting that the nephew is primarily concerned with the idea of lack, the absence of the *'objet petit autre,'* and with the illusion of presence which language creates.

The 'little other' illustrates for the child the idea of lack, loss, and absence, showing the child that it isn't complete in and of itself. It is also the gateway to the Symbolic Order, to language, since language itself is premised on the idea of lack or absence, and since language, in providing the signifier 'I' which solidifies the mirror image as the signified, the self, compensates for lack by creating an illusion of full presence for the speaking subject who believes language comes from her or his self.

Lacan says these ideas of other and Other, of lack and absence and 'I'dentity and the (mis)identification of self with o/Other, are all worked out on an individual level with each child, but they form the basic structures of the Symbolic Order, of language, which the child must enter in order to become an adult member of culture, a self-in-language. Thus the otherness acted out in the fort/da game, as well as in the distinctions made in the mirror phase between self and other, become categorical or structural ideas.

The Other, with a capital 'O,' is a structural position in the Symbolic Order. It is the place that everyone is trying to get to, to merge with, in order to get rid of the separation between 'self' and 'other.' It is, in Derrida's sense, the *center* of the system, the center of the Symbolic and/or the center of language itself as structure. As such, the Other is the thing to which every element relates. But as the center, the Other (again, not a person but a position) can't be merged with. Nothing can be in the center with the Other, even though everything in the system, like people, want to be. So the position of the Other creates and sustains a never-ending lack, which Lacan calls *desire*. This desire is the desire to be the Other. By definition, desire can never be fulfilled: it's not desire for some object (which would be need) or desire for love or another person's recognition of oneself (which would be demand) but desire to be the center of the system, the center of the Symbolic order.

This center has lots of names in Lacanian theory. It's the Other; it's also called the *Phallus*. Lacan here borrows again from Freud's original Oedipus theory. The mirror stage is pre-oedipal. The self is constructed in relation to an other, to the idea of Other, and the self wants to merge with the Other. As in Freud's world, the most important other in a child's life is its mother, so the child wants to merge with its mother. In Lacan's terms, this is the child's demand that the self/other split be erased. The child decides that it can merge with the mother if it becomes what the mother wants it to be – in Lacan's terms, the child tries to fulfill the mother's desire. The mother's desire, formed by her own entry into the Symbolic, because she is already a language-using adult 'self,' is not to have lack, or Lack – the mother desires to be the Other, the place where nothing is lacking. This fits with the Freudian version of the Oedipus Complex, where the child wants to merge with its mother by having sexual intercourse with her. In Freud's model, the idea of lack is represented by the lack of a penis. The boy who wants to sleep with his mother wants to complete her lack by filling her up with his penis.

In Freud's view, what breaks up this oedipal desire – for boys, anyway – is the father, who threatens castration. The father threatens to make the boy experience lack, the absence of the penis, if he tries to use his penis to make up for his mother's lack of a penis. In

LITERARY THEORY: A GUIDE FOR THE PERPLEXED

Lacan's terms, the threat of castration is a metaphor for the whole idea of Lack as a structural concept. For Lacan, it isn't the real father who threatens castration. Rather, because the idea of lack, or Lack, is essential to the concept of language, because the concept of Lack is part of the basic structuration of language, the father becomes a function of the linguistic structure. The Father, rather than being a person, a small-o other, becomes a structuring principle of the Symbolic.

For Lacan, Freud's angry father becomes the Name-of-the-Father, or the Law-of-the-Father, or sometimes just the Law. Submission to the rules of language itself – to the Law of the Father – is required in order to enter into the Symbolic order. To become a speaking language-using subject, you have to be subjected to, you have to obey, the laws and rules of language. Lacan designates the idea of the structure of language and its rules as specifically paternal. He calls the rules of language the Law-of-the-Father in order to link the entry into the Symbolic, into the structure of language, to Freud's notion of the Oedipus and Castration Complexes, and to the creation of the superego.

The Law-of-the-Father, or Name-of-the-Father, is another term for the Other, for the center of the Symbolic, the thing that governs the whole structure and determines how all the elements in the system can move and form relationships. This center is also called the Phallus to underline even more the patriarchal nature of the Symbolic Order. The Phallus, as center, limits the play of elements and gives stability to the whole structure. The Phallus anchors the chain of signifiers which, in the unconscious, are just floating and sliding and shifting. The Phallus stops play, so that signifiers can be connected firmly to signifieds. It is because the Phallus is the center of the Symbolic Order, the center of language, that the term 'I' designates the idea of the self, and why any word has relatively stable meaning.

The Phallus is not the same as the penis. Penises belong to individuals; the Phallus belongs to the structure of language itself. No one has it, just like no one governs language or rules language. The Phallus is the center. It's what governs the whole structure, it's what everyone wants to be, or to have, but no one can get there – as Derrida said, no element of the system can take the place of the center. That's what Lacan calls 'Desire:' the desire, which can never be satisfied, to be the center and to rule the system.

Lacan says that boys think they have a chance to be the Phallus and occupy the position of center because they have penises. Girls have a harder time misperceiving themselves as eligible to be the Phallus because they are, as Freud says, constituted by and as lack. The binary oppositions that structure Western thought associate boys with penis, presence, and order, while girls are associated with lack of penis, absence, and disorder. The Phallus is the place where there is no lack, hence girls have a tougher time believing they can be the Phallus. Lacan insists, however, that no one can be the Phallus; every subject in language, every person who enters the Symbolic order and becomes a speaking subject, is constituted by and as lack. The only reason we have language at all is because of the loss, or lack, of the union with the maternal body. It is the necessity to become an adult, part of culture, to have language, that forces everyone to be defined by absence, loss, and lack. But Western philosophy values presence so thoroughly that we go to almost any length to mask the awareness that our civilization itself depends upon lack.

The anatomical distinction between the sexes is significant in Lacan's psychoanalysis, though not in the same way it is in Freud's. Lacan talks about this in his essay 'The Agency of the Letter in the Unconscious.' He makes two drawings in that essay: the first is the word 'tree' over a picture of a tree, which is the classic Saussurean concept of signifier (word) and signified (object). But then he adds a second drawing, of two identical doors. Over one door is the word 'Ladies' and over the other is the word 'Gentlemen.' Here's a complication to Saussure's signifier–signified connection, where identical signifieds have two completely different signifiers.

Lacan explains the door drawing this way:

> A train arrives at a station. A little boy and a little girl, brother and sister, are seated in a compartment face to face next to the window through which the buildings along the station platform can be seen passing as the train pulls to a stop. 'Look,' says the brother, 'we're at Ladies!' 'Idiot!' replies his sister, 'Can't you see we're at Gentlemen?'[7]

This anecdote shows how boys and girls enter the Symbolic order, the structure of language, differently. In Lacan's view, each child can see only the signifier of the other gender; each child constructs its world-view, its understanding of the relation between signifier and signified, as the consequence of seeing an 'other.' As Lacan puts it, 'For these children, Ladies and Gentlemen will be henceforth two countries toward which each of their souls will strive on divergent wings.'[8] Each child, each sex, can only see, or signify, the otherness of the other sex. You might take Lacan's drawing of the two doors literally: these are the doors, with their gender distinctions, through which each child must pass in order to enter into the Symbolic realm.

In taking up a position in the Symbolic, you enter through a gender-marked doorway; the position girls occupy in the structure of language, in relation to the Phallus, is different than the position for boys. Boys are closer to the Phallus than girls, but no one is or has the Phallus, since it's the center. Your position in the Symbolic, like the position of all other signifying elements, is fixed by the Phallus, held in place by the center. Unlike in the unconscious, the chains of signifiers in the Symbolic don't circulate and slide endlessly because the Phallus limits play.

Paradoxically – as if all this wasn't confusing enough! – the Phallus and the Real are pretty similar. Both are places where things are whole, complete, full, unified, where there's no lack and no Lack. Both are places that are inaccessible to the human subject-in-language. But they are also opposite: the Real is the maternal, the ground from which we spring, the nature we have to separate from in order to have culture; the Phallus is the idea of the Father, the patriarchal order of culture, the position which rules everything in the world.

As you might imagine, feminist theorists have a lot to say about Freud and Lacan's versions of psychoanalysis, a topic which we'll take up in the next chapter.

## NOTES

1  Sigmund Freud, *Three Essays on the Theory of Sexuality*. New York: HarperCollins, 1962, p. 85.
2  *Ibid.*, p. 87.
3  Sigmund Freud, 'Some Psychological Consequences of the Anatomical Distinction Between the Sexes,' in *Standard Edition of the Collected Works of Sigmund Freud*, ed. James Strachey. London: Hogarth Press, 1964, p. 191.
4  *Ibid.*, p. 195.
5  Freud, 'The Question of Lay Analysis,' in *Standard Edition*, vol. XX, p. 134.
6  Freud, 'The Dissection of the Psychical Personality,' in *Standard Edition*, vol. XXII, p. 80.

7  Jacques Lacan, 'The Agency of the Letter in the Unconscious, or, Reason Since Freud,' in Hazard Adams and Leroy Searle, eds, *Critical Theory Since 1965*. Gainesville, FL: University Press of Florida, 1986, p. 742.
8  *Ibid.*, p. 742.

## SUGGESTIONS FOR FURTHER READING

Richard Appignanesi, *Introducing Freud*. New York: Totem Books, 1999.
Sean Homer, *Jacques Lacan*. New York: Routledge, 2005.
Richard Osborne, Maurice Mechan, *Freud for Beginners*. New York: Writers and Readers Publishing Inc., 1993.
Ivan Ward, *Introducing Psychoanalysis*. New York: Totem Books, 2000.

# INTERLUDE: 'SELF' TO 'SUBJECT'

Before we launch into the second half of the book, let's review where we are and how we've arrived here.

In reading structuralist theory, we've started to ask questions about the way words make meaning, about the structure of language itself, about the relationship between signifier and signified, and about the idea of negative value and difference. In poststructuralist theory, such as deconstruction, we've been asking questions about binary oppositions and how such binary oppositions structure the way we perceive, think about, and act in our world. We've also begun to look at what would happen if the binary oppositions fell apart, and if the systems of which they are the basis began to shake, totter, and collapse.

In psychoanalytic theories, we've been asking questions about the idea of a 'self,' about how identity – or 'I'dentity – is formed, and about the relationship between the conscious mind, the ego, and the unconscious. Central to these questions has been understanding the binary opposition 'self'/'other,' how it's been constructed and maintained, and what happens when that particular binary is deconstructed. We've also begun, through psychoanalytic theories, to open up questions about the role that sex and gender play in the construction of an 'I'dentity.

In all of these questions and kinds of theorizing, we've had to throw out (or at least put away) some of our most cherished ideas from the humanist tradition and to replace them with the fundamental premises of poststructuralist thought, including these ideas:

- 'Identity' or selfhood is not something natural, essential, or innate, but rather is something that is socially *constructed*.

- What is constructed can be changed, put into play, destabilized, altered, and reworked.
- 'Self' is a concept constructed from and within language; self-hood is an illusion produced by language; language is an impersonal structure which we inhabit; language speaks us.
- The entity which inhabits the structure of language is subjected to the rules and limitations of language, and the concept of 'self' is a misrecognition of one's position as a subject in language.
- Determinate meaning in language is a product of, and the illusion of, a structure stabilized by a center, which limits play, tries to limit meaning, and which subjects all language-using subjects to its rules.

In the humanist model, the 'self' was defined as a conscious being who had the power of logic and rationality to discover the truth about the workings of the world, and who was able to act and think for himself or herself, independently of external influences, and also able to think reflexively about the status of his or her own being. The poststructuralist notion of 'subject' radically decenters the idea of 'self,' stripping it of its autonomy and its ability to deduce 'truth.' Here's a brief discussion of how the shift from self to subject changes the way we think about literary studies.

Under the humanist mode, an *author*, an original creative self, could write *literature*, which was a product of her unique experiences and expressions, using language which she originated and used with conscious intention to create layers of meaning. The *reader*, or interpreting self, could understand the author's text, work to interpret her meaning, and usually would incorporate some part of the author's meaning as a kind of truth.

Within the poststructuralist model, language as structure produces *subjects*, who write, speak, and use signs, but only as the vehicle through which language works, rather than as original creative beings; and *texts*, which are combinations of signs or signifiers which pre-exist any particular subject, and which are the units in the structure of language which are combined according to the structure's rules (grammar) to create meaning.

Subjects inhabit a wide variety of positions within the structure of language. I find it useful to think of a large lecture room or auditorium, where the seats are bolted to the floor in rows. Each seat is a subject position within the structure. You can move from one seat to another and inhabit a different position in relation to the 'center' (the stage or platform which all the seats face), and each seat gives you a different perspective on or experience of the center – but all the seats are fixed, and it doesn't matter which individual subject occupies which seat. In poststructuralist literary theory, some of the seats or subject positions in language have specific designations, such as *author* and *reader*, but these positions or seats are no different from any other subject position within the structure of language (what Lacan calls the *Symbolic Order*).

Texts, as microcosms of language, as subsystems created by and with the same structure as language, also produce subject positions; these are the positions which the text opens for readers to position themselves in relation to the text. An example of a subject position might be when a text addresses the reader directly, using 'you' (as I've done in this book). 'You' is a signifier that denotes the position any possible reader may occupy. Texts also designate readerly subject positions through devices like point of view; such positioning governs a subject's range of interpretation, just as the structure of language governs a subject's possible speech.

Subject positions vary from text to text. A reader's ability to occupy the subject positions made available by a text also varies, depending on what kind of subject the text is asking for. A reader's subject position is determined by a variety of factors: the 'seat' you occupy in the classroom or auditorium depends to some degree on your age, race, gender, social position, educational level, and other markers of difference. While all 'selves,' in the humanist tradition, may be created equal, and considered as identical because all selves share the same essential characteristics, such as reason and free will, no two 'subjects' are alike. Indeed, like any element in a structure, a subject's specific positioning within the structure will be based at least in part on its differences from all the other subject positions within the structure.

# CHAPTER 6

# FEMINISM

Lacan pointed out that the entry into the Symbolic Order, the structure of language, is different for boys and girls; gender is yet another element that determines subject position. Poststructuralist feminist theories examine how gender is socially constructed, rather than natural, innate, or essential; they also see gender as the product of, or an illusion created by, the same structures of language that create the illusion of the 'I'dentity.

Theories examining gender existed long before poststructuralist thought. Gender is a cultural universal: all societies mark gender distinctions in some way, though of course all societies make those markings differently. Feminists since the Middle Ages have been asking whether gender is biological or cultural, whether it is innate and natural and God-given, or whether it is socially constructed and therefore mutable. Is anatomy destiny, as Freud asserted, so that genetics, biology, morphology, physiology, and brain chemistry determine social roles for men and women, so that what is biologically male is by definition inalterably masculine, and what is biologically female is by definition feminine? Or – and most feminists favor this answer – is gender socially constructed, therefore variable, mutable, and not necessarily tied to anatomical or genetic determinants?

It's worth noting, in passing, that scientific studies about gender in relation to genetics and chemistry and brain structure tend to say that gender is both: it's enormously mutable, but there does seem to be something that might be essential. This topic is worth investigating further.

Poststructuralist cultural theorists of gender, on the other hand, say that gender is a set of signifiers attached to sexually dimorphic bodies, and that these signifiers work to divide social practices and relations into the binary oppositions of male/female and masculine/feminine. You might think here about high heels as a signifier: generally, a foot in a high-heeled shoe signifies that there's a vagina and breasts attached to the wearer, because in our culture high heels are a signifier of femaleness and femininity. But anyone *can* wear high heels – and will be seen as 'feminine' because of it. You might also think about recent studies concerning the variety of sex markers: genetics and physiology allow for several different ways of determining sex, including chromosomal sex, presence of external genitalia (penis or clitoris), presence of internal reproductive organs (testes or ovaries), hormonal sex (predominance of testosterone or estrogen), muscular and skeletal structure, and brain structure. It's possible for any individual to have some of the markers for one sex and some of the markers for the other sex, thus deconstructing the binary opposition of male/female on which Western cultural constructions of sex and gender identity rely. This is why Western medicine, when it encounters a newborn with ambiguous or multiple sex or gender markings, works to eliminate the anomalous ones through surgery or hormonal treatment, in order to assign each newborn to one of the two binary categories that our culture recognizes.

From a poststructuralist viewpoint,

- 'Gender' is a relationship established between signifiers, things that signal gender, and signifieds, taken to be the physical sex of the person. Like all signifier–signified connections, this relationship is *arbitrary*.
- 'Gender' operates within Western constructs of binary opposites, so that gender signifiers always point to either a male or female body, and to masculine or feminine traits.
- Since 'gender' is constructed through arbitrary links between signifiers and signifieds, the connection between the two can be weakened, changed, or broken. Since the signifiers of gender help maintain the system of binary oppositions that shape Western thought by dividing the world into 'male' and 'female,' and valuing 'male' over 'female,' gender can be deconstructed, and the elements that constitute stable notions of gender can be put into play.

Feminist theories, examining how gender is constructed, can be found in virtually every discipline within the university, including the hard sciences and mathematics; it's certainly a prominent part of the conversations occurring in the social sciences and humanities. Academic disciplines have embraced feminist theories in part as pure knowledge, for the same reason we embrace any kind of theory: because the theory explains something we want or need to know.

But feminist theory, like most poststructuralist theories, also has a political dimension as well. That political dimension consists, at the very least, of an awareness of the power imbalances enforced and upheld by the inequalities in the binary oppositions which structure how we think about and act in our world. Even more than just an 'awareness' of these imbalances and inequalities, feminist theories provide analyses of how these inequalities evolved, how they operate, and – perhaps most importantly and also most controversially – how they might, could, should be changed in order to create a more equitable arrangement of social power and privilege. It is this last element – the element of social change, of political advocacy – that generally makes people uncomfortable with the idea of feminist theory as an academic or intellectual pursuit.

In this chapter, we'll be looking at two strands of feminist theory which have direct ties to literary study: an Anglo-American strand that emerges from the humanist tradition, and a poststructuralist strand that questions the assumptions and premises of the humanist model.

## 'PRE-POSTSTRUCTURALIST' FEMINIST LITERARY THEORY

One of the books I picked up in a Boston bookstore in 1980, just when I had graduated from college, was *The Madwoman in the Attic*, by Sandra Gilbert and Susan Gubar. It examines the works of major nineteenth-century women writers, including Jane Austen, Mary Shelley, Emily Bronte, Charlotte Bronte, George Eliot, and Emily Dickinson, all women writers whose works I had studied – in my only course on women writers – in my undergraduate English major. I was eager to read it, both to expand my knowledge of these authors and the contexts in which they wrote, and to feel that self-congratulatory sense of being able to tackle, and enjoy, a work designed for professional literary scholars.

It was – and is – an exemplary text, one which in 1980 was by far the most sophisticated intellectual example of feminist literary criticism, and which today remains an important landmark in the evolution of feminist criticism. The first section, 'Toward a Feminist Poetics,' presents a theory of women's writing which examines the difficulty the Western literary tradition has had in allowing the two words 'woman' and 'writer' to be joined together. Specifically, Gilbert and Gubar question the metaphors which have shaped the practice of writing and the idea of creativity, noting that masculine imagery has completely dominated Western thinking about authors and texts. 'Is the pen a metaphorical penis?' they ask in the book's first sentence.[1] Their feminist literary theory revolves around investigating how the equation 'pen = penis' has limited women writers. They begin by documenting exhaustively the extent of this equation in Western literary history, showing that pen = penis has been the dominant metaphor for all acts of literary creation since at least the Middle Ages. They argue that the predominance of this metaphor relies on the idea that women's bodies give birth to babies, which are mortal and limited, while men's bodies 'give birth' to immortal things, like books and art.

Exploring the reasons for this association of male bodies with immortal births, Gilbert and Gubar offer a variety of possible causes: it might be an anxious response to the male inability to know for sure that they are really the father of the children their wives have; it might be a reaction to the threat of castration (in Freudian terms) by asserting the predominance and presence of the penis as the creative organ; it might be a conscious attempt on the part of male authors deliberately to exclude women writers from membership in their exclusive club by defining the only 'good' writing as writing done by men. Gilbert and Gubar particularly read it as an attempt to reduce what Harold Bloom calls 'the anxiety of influence,' the feeling that one will never be as good as one's father, one's literary forebears.

Having documented the dominance of the idea that male bodies and male sexuality alone form the metaphoric basis for acts of creativity, including writing, in the Western cultural imagination, Gilbert and Gubar then ask, 'With what organ can females generate texts?'[2] The exclusion of women from the biologically-given tools of the trade means that women writers have had to find alternate methods and materials of writing. The rest of their excellent book examines nineteenth-century British and American women writers to find how they constructed their practices of writing, both metaphorically and literally. Did they use milk, or blood, instead of ink, and write on bark or cloth instead of paper? Gilbert and Gubar began the feminist search for what was made invisible by the patriarchal tradition of 'pen = penis,' urging feminist scholars to look for women's writing in places, and using instruments, not usually associated with writing.

Most Anglo-American feminist literary theory – before the deluge of poststructuralist theories which flooded British and American universities in the 1980s and 1990s – followed the same kind of humanist lines of thought and inquiry epitomized in Gilbert and Gubar's germinal work. This branch of theory asks questions about how women writers were discouraged or prevented from publishing their writings, or writing at all; it seeks to explain why there are so few women writers in the Western canon of literature in English. Finding answers to these questions sparked a vitally important historical search for 'forgotten' women writers, and prompted feminist literary critics to challenge the aesthetic and political standards on which that Western canon was based. Anglo-American feminist literary theory and criticism radically rewrote the ways we think about the history of literature in English, adding countless texts by women (and by other under-represented groups) to the lists and successfully altering the standards by which literary excellence (hence canonicity) was evaluated. The result has been the development of a canon – reflected in anthologies of literature, courses in literature, and in numerous volumes of literary criticism – which has learned to value the works of women writers, and to re-evaluate the works of male writers in light of the issues raised by women writers and feminist criticism.

## POSTSTRUCTURALIST FEMINIST LITERARY THEORY

The Anglo-American feminist literary critical approach, however, was limited by its humanist roots and paradigms. While Gilbert and Gubar make a new space for women writers to be celebrated as 'mothers' of texts, equal in importance to the 'fathers' of the Western tradition, they did not question the humanist ideal that the author is an original creator. Though they questioned how gender affected the practice of writing in its social and historical aspects, they did not think about whether gender shaped the structure of language itself, and the individual subject's access to that structure. It took the advent of poststructuralist thinking, particularly coming from intellectual feminists in Paris, to spark the development of poststructuralist feminist theories of women and writing.

The other book I picked up in the bookstore on that eventful day in 1980 was *New French Feminisms*, edited by Elaine Marks and Isabel de Courtivron. It contained essays, most of them short excerpts of longer works, by theorists I'd never heard of, including Hélène Cixous, Luce Irigaray, and Julia Kristeva. I couldn't understand a word of what they were talking about. Though I prided myself on being a feminist, nothing in my humanist undergraduate English major had prepared me to comprehend feminist theory, which was based on the poststructuralist ideas of Saussure, Derrida, and Lacan – none of whom I'd ever heard of either. After trying to read a few pages, I threw the book across the room in frustration. Then I picked it up and took it with me to graduate school to see if someone there could explain it.

Poststructuralist feminist theory isn't about women. Rather, it's about 'woman' and 'man' as subject positions within the structure of language, positions that Lacan hints at in his example of the boy and girl arriving at 'Ladies' and 'Gentlemen.' Poststructuralist feminist theory sees the category or position 'woman' as part of a binary opposition, 'man/woman,' in which 'man' is the favored term; feminist theories then want to deconstruct that binary, and the other binaries which reinforce and maintain it, including masculine/feminine, good/evil, light/dark, positive/negative, culture/nature, etc. All the things on the right side of the slash are things Western culture works to control, to suppress, or to exclude, positing them as disruptive or destructive to the concepts on the left side of the slash. Poststructuralist feminist theory investigates how, and with what consequences, 'woman' is constructed as otherness, as non-being, as alterity, as something outside of and dangerous to consciousness, rationality, presence, and all those other nice things that Western humanist metaphysics values.

All of this comes from Lacan's idea that woman is 'not All' – that the position of 'woman' in the Symbolic is founded on Lack, so that 'woman' can't (mis)identify with the Phallus as the center of the Symbolic Order. 'Woman' is a subject position on the edge of the Symbolic, not firmly governed by the center, and hence there's something in that position that 'escapes discourse,' that is not fully controlled by the center and the structure of language.

It may be useful here to think again of a lecture room with fixed seats, or an auditorium or theater. The seats are subject positions you occupy when you enter the theater. You have a ticket – a signifier or set of signifiers – that directs you to your particular seat, your particular position within the structure. Your ticket can specify a wide range of signifiers that can determine your position. For instance, your ticket may say 'woman,' and thus your seat will be at the back of the theater, away from the center, or center stage. Your ticket may say 'upper class,' in which case your seat will be closer to the center. The signifiers on your ticket can be contradictory – your ticket may say 'woman,' 'African-American,' and 'medical doctor,' in which case your seating position would be further away from the stage for the less-valued signifiers (woman, African-American) but closer to the stage for the more valued signifier (medical doctor). Your ticket can even direct you to a seat not indicated by your physical being: a biological female may hold a ticket that says 'man' or 'masculine,' and thus get to sit closer to the stage, and a biological male may hold a ticket that says 'woman' or 'feminine,' and thus sit further away.

According to poststructuralist feminist theorists, subjects who are further away from the controlling influence of the center have more play, more 'freedom' to move and to behave as they wish. The capacity to avoid, escape, or evade the structuring rules of the center of a structure or system is what Lacan and the poststructuralist feminist theorists call *jouissance* which is the French word for 'orgasm.' The word in poststructuralist terminology means a pleasure that is beyond language, beyond discourse, something that can't be expressed in words or in the structure of language, and which in fact is disruptive to that structure. This form of pleasure, or any activity or position that escapes the rules and structures held in place by the Phallus, is a specifically feminine pleasure, a feminine *jouissance* which is unrepresentable in language, and which interrupts representation, disturbs the linear flow of language, and rattles the foundations of the structure of the Symbolic. Thus *jouissance* can be considered a type of deconstruction, as it shakes up the fixity and stability of the structure of language and puts signifiers into play, making them slippery and indeterminate.

Poststructuralist feminist theory generally equates this feminine *jouissance* with the female body, with the state of 'nature' and the Real which the infant must abandon in order to enter the Symbolic Order and take up a subject position in language. In this sense, poststructuralist feminist theory is asking the same question Gilbert and Gubar ask: Is women's writing, or women's language, somehow related to female bodies and female biology? If so, how?

## HÉLÈNE CIXOUS AND 'THE LAUGH OF THE MEDUSA'

Hélène Cixous take up where Lacan left off, noting that women and men enter into the Symbolic Order in different ways, or through different doors, and that the subject positions open to either sex within the Symbolic are also different. She understands that, when Lacan calls the center of the Symbolic Order the Phallus, he highlights what a patriarchal system language is – or, more specifically, what a *phallogocentric* system it is. This word is the combination of two words and two ideas: 'phallocentric,' meaning 'centered around the phallus,' which describes Lacan's notion of the structure of language, and 'logocentric,' which is Derrida's term to describe Western culture's preference for speech over language, for logic and rationality over madness, and for all the other binary oppositions which shape our metaphysics. Cixous combines the two words to describe Western cultural structures as 'phallogocentric,' based on the primacy of the terms on the left-hand side of the slash in any array of binary opposites. A phallogocentric culture is one which aligns all the left-side terms as the valued ones, and consigns the right-side terms to the position of 'other' or undesirable.

Cixous follows Lacan's psychoanalytic paradigm, which argues that a child must separate from its mother's body – the Real – in order to enter into the Symbolic. Because of this, Cixous says, the female body in general becomes unrepresentable in language; it's what can't be spoken or written in the phallogocentric Symbolic order. Cixous here makes a leap from the maternal body to the female body in general; she also leaps from that female body to female sexuality, saying that female sexuality, female *jouissance*, is unrepresentable, unspeakable, in the phallogocentric Symbolic Order.

To understand how she makes this leap, we have to go back to what Freud says about female sexuality, and the mess he makes of it. In Freud's story of the female Oedipus Complex, girls have to make a lot of switches, from clitoris to vagina, from attraction to female bodies to attraction to male bodies, and from active ('masculine') sexuality to passive ('feminine') sexuality, in order to become 'normal' (non-incestuous reproductive heterosexual) adults. Cixous rewrites this, via Lacan, by pointing out that 'adult-hood' in Lacan's terms is the same as entry into the Symbolic Order and taking up a subject position. For a woman, becoming a linguistic subject always means having only one kind of sexuality: passive, vaginal, heterosexual, reproductive. And that sexuality, if one follows Freud to his logical extreme, is not a 'female' sexuality per se, but always a sexuality defined and described in male/masculine terms: the woman's pleasure is to come from being passively filled by a penis. So, Cixous concludes, there really isn't any such thing as female sexuality in and of itself in a phallogocentric system: it's always a sexuality defined by the presence (or absence) of a penis, and not by anything intrinsic to the female body or female sexual pleasure.

If women have to be forced away from their own bodies – first in the person of the mother's body, and then in the person of their unique sexual feelings and pleasures – in order to assume a subject position in language, is it possible, Cixous asks, for a woman to write or speak at all? Is it possible for a woman to write as a woman, or is her subject position within the Symbolic necessarily a renunciation of all that is 'woman' in favor of all that is 'man?' Does a woman who writes or speaks do so from a masculine position? If the structure of language itself is phallogocentric, and stable meaning – the seemingly firm connection between a single signifier and a single signified – is anchored and guaranteed by the Phallus, then isn't everyone who uses language taking up a position as 'male' within this structure which by definition excludes the female body?

Cixous and other poststructuralist feminists are both outraged and intrigued by the possibilities for relations between gender and writing (or language use in general) opened up by Lacan's paradigms. In 'The Laugh of the Medusa,' Cixous states that her project has two aims: to break up and destroy, and to foresee and project. She wants to destroy (or perhaps deconstruct) the phallogocentric system Lacan describes, and to project some new strategies for a new kind of relation between female bodies and language.

Lacan's description of the Symbolic, as illustrated in his drawing of the two identical doors (signfieds) attached to different signifiers, places men and women in different positions within the Symbolic in relation to the Phallus; men more easily misperceive themselves as having the Phallus, or being closer to it, whereas women, who instead of penises have 'nothing,' have 'absence,' according to Freud, are further away from the center. Poststructuralist feminist theories argue that women are thus closer to the margins of the Symbolic order, and are not as rigidly held in place by the rule of the center, or what Lacan also calls the 'Law-of-the-Father.' Using the theater metaphor, women sit in the back row, closer to the door and further from the organizing center of the stage; from that back row, they have more freedom to behave as they choose, rather than as the center dictates. They are also closer to the Imaginary, to images and fantasies, and further from the idea of absolute fixed and stable meaning than men are.

Because women are less fixed in stable positions within the Symbolic than men, women and their language are more fluid, more flowing, more flexible than men and their language. It is worth noting here that when Cixous talks about 'women' and 'woman,' sometimes she means the terms literally, denoting the physical beings with vaginas and breasts, and sometimes she uses the terms to denote the linguistic structural position: 'woman' is a signifier in the chain of signifiers within the Symbolic, just as 'man' is (and 'chair' and 'dog' and 'computer,' for that matter). Any signifier has stable meaning – 'woman' is the signifier connected to the signified of vagina, breasts, etc. – because it is locked in place, anchored, by the center of the system, which limits play. When Cixous says that woman is more slippery, more fluid, less fixed, and more playful than man, she means both the literal woman, the person, and the signifier 'woman.' Here's where the line between biology or physiology and subject position gets blurred again. Is Cixous arguing, like Freud, that anatomy is destiny in language?

Cixous's essay, like most of those written from a poststructuralist perspective, is difficult to understand, not only because she assumes we all know Freud's and Lacan's formulations about female sexuality and the structure of language, but also because she writes on two levels at once: she is always being both metaphoric and literal, referring both to structures and to real people. When she says that 'woman must write herself,' and 'woman must write woman,' she means both that women must write themselves, tell their own stories, and that 'woman' as signifier must have a new way to be connected to the signifier 'I,' and to write the signifier of selfhood or subjecthood offered within the Symbolic Order.

Cixous also discusses writing on both a metaphoric and a literal level. She aligns writing with masturbation, something that for women is supposed to be secret, shameful, or silly, something not quite grown-up, something that will be renounced in order to achieve full adulthood, just as clitoral stimulation has to be renounced in favor of vaginal reproductive passive adult sexuality. If men write with their penises, as Gilbert and Gubar argue, then Cixous says that before women can write they have to discover where their sexual pleasure is located.

Cixous also argues that men haven't yet discovered the relation between their sexuality and their writing, as long as they are focused on writing with the penis. 'Man must write man,' Cixous says, again focusing on 'man' as a signifier within the Symbolic, which is no more privileged that 'woman' as a signifier. Cixous explains that men's sexuality, like women's, has always been defined and circumscribed by binary oppositions (active/passive, masculine/feminine), and that heterosexual relations have been structured by a sense of otherness and fear created by these absolute binaries. As long as male sexuality is defined in these limited and limiting terms, Cixous says, men will be prisoners of a Symbolic Order which alienates them from their bodies in ways similar to (though not identical with) how women are alienated from their bodies and their sexualities. Thus, while Cixous does slam men directly for being patriarchal oppressors, she also identifies the structures which enforce gender dichotomies as being oppressive to both sexes.

She also links these oppressive binary structures to other Western cultural practices, particularly those involving racial distinctions. She follows Freud in calling women 'the dark continent,' and expands the metaphor by reference to apartheid to demonstrate that these same binary systems which structure gender also structure imperialism: women are aligned with darkness, with otherness, with Africa, against men who are aligned with lightness, with selfhood, and with Western civilization. In writing about this, Cixous refers to women as 'they,' as if women are non-speakers, non-writers, whom she is observing: 'As soon as they begin to speak, at the same time as they're taught their name, they can be taught that their territory is black.'[3] As soon as women (or any other 'other') enters the Symbolic and takes up a subject position, they are assigned a name and told the meaning of their particular position.

Cixous argues that most women do write and speak, but that they do so from a 'masculine' position; in order to speak, woman has assumed she needs a stable system of meaning, and thus has aligned herself with the Phallus, which anchors language. There has been little or no 'feminine' writing, Cixous says. In making this statement, she insists that writing is always 'marked' within a Symbolic Order that is structured through binary oppositions, including 'masculine/ feminine,' in which the feminine is always repressed. Cixous coins the term *'l'ecriture feminine'* to refer to this notion of feminine writing, with masculine writing as its phallogocentric counterpart. She sees *l'ecriture feminine* first of all as something possible only in poetry, in terms of existing literary genres, and not in realist prose. Novels, she says, are 'allies of representationalism;' they are genres, which try to speak in stable language, language where one signifier points to one signified. In poetry, however, language is set free – the chains of signifiers flow more freely, and meaning is less determinate. Poetry, according to Cixous, is closer to the unconscious, which, as Lacan describes, is structured like chains of signifiers which never rest, never attach to any signified. Being closer to the unconscious, poetry is also closer to what has been repressed into the unconscious, which is female sexuality and the female body. It is worth noting, however, that though Cixous claims poetry as a form of *l'ecriture feminine*, all the poets she cites as feminine writers are men.

Such feminine writing will serve as a rupture, or a site of transformation and change, Cixous claims. She means 'rupture' here in the same sense as Derrida, a place where the totality of the system breaks down and one can see a system as a system, rather than simply as 'the truth.' Feminine writing will show the phallogocentric structure of the Symbolic as something constructed, not as something inevitable and essential, and thus allow us to deconstruct that order.

There are two levels on which *l'ecriture feminine* will be transformative, according to Cixous, and these levels correspond again to her use of the literal and the metaphoric, or the individual and the structural. On one level, the individual woman must write herself, must discover for herself what her body feels like, and how to write about that body in language. Specifically, women must find their own sexuality, one that is rooted solely in their own bodies, and find ways to write about that pleasure, that *jouissance*. On the second level, when women speak or write their own bodies, the structure of language itself will change; as women become active subjects, not just beings passively acted upon, their position as subject in language will shift. Women who write – if they don't merely reproduce the phallogocentric system of stable ordered meaning which already exists, and which excludes them as women – will be creating a new signifying system, which will have built into it far more play, more fluidity, than the existing rigid phallogocentric Symbolic Order. This writing will be more like poetry than prose, and its meanings will be multiple and ambiguous, rather than clear and rational, based on the attachment of signifier to signified. 'Beware, my friend,' Cixous writes toward the end of the essay, 'of the signifier that would take you back to the authority of a signified!'[4]

The woman who speaks, Cixous says, and who does not reproduce the representational stability of the Symbolic Order, will not speak in linear fasion, will not 'make sense' in any currently existing form. *L'ecriture feminine*, like feminine speech, will not be objective or objectifiable; it will erase the divisions between speech and text, between order and chaos, between sense and nonsense. In this way, *l'ecriture feminine* will be an inherently deconstructive language. Such speech/writing (and remember, this language will erase the slash) will bring users closer to the realm of the Real, back to the mother's body, to the breast, to the sense of union or non-separation. This is why Cixous uses the metaphor of 'white ink,' of writing in breast milk; she wants to convey the idea of a reunion with the maternal body, to a place where there is no lack or separation.

Cixous's description of what *l'ecriture feminine* looks like – or, better, what it sounds like, since it's not clear that this writing will 'look like' anything, as 'looking like' is at the heart of the misperception of self in the mirror stage which launches one into the Symbolic Order – flows into metaphor, which she also means literally. She wants to be careful to talk about writing in new ways, in ways that distinguish *l'ecriture feminine* from existing forms of speech or writing, and in so doing she associates feminine writing with existing non-linguistic modes. *L'ecriture feminine* is milk, it's a song, it's something with rhythm and pulse, but no words, something connected with bodies and with bodies' beats and movements, but not with representational language.

She uses these metaphors also to be 'slippery,' arguing that one can't define the practice of *l'ecriture feminine*. To define something is to pin it down, to anchor it, to limit it, to put it in its place within a stable system or structure – and Cixous says that *l'ecriture feminine* is too fluid for that; it will always resist, exceed, or escape any definition. It can't be theorized, enclosed, encoded, or understood – which doesn't mean, she warns, that it doesn't exist. Rather, it will always be greater than the existing systems for classification and ordering of knowledge in phallogocentric Western culture. It can't be defined, but it can be 'conceived of' – another phrase which works on both literal and metaphoric levels – by subjects not subjugated to a central authority. Only those on the margins, the 'outlaws,' can 'conceive of' feminine language; those outlaws will be women, and anyone else who can resist or be distanced from the structuring central Phallus of the phallogocentric Symbolic Order.

In discussing who might exist in the position of outlaw, Cixous brings up the question of bisexuality. Again, she starts from Freud's idea that all humans are fundamentally bisexual, and that the Oedipal trajectory which steers both boys and girls into hetero-sexuality is an unfortunate requirement of culture. For Cixous, 'culture' is always a phallogocentric order; the entry into the Symbolic requires the division between male and female, masculine and feminine, which subordinates and represses the feminine. By erasing or deconstructing the slash between masculine and femin-ine, however, Cixous is not arguing for Freud's old idea of bisexu-ality. Rather, she wants a new bisexuality, the 'other bisexuality,' which is the 'nonexclusion either of the difference of one sex' – a refusal of self/other as a structuring dichotomy.[5] In essence, rather than taping masculine and feminine together, Cixous's bisexuality would dissolve the distinctions, so that sexuality would be from any body, any body part, at any time; it would be more like the poly-morphous perversity that Freud says all infants have, but which has to be organized and disciplined in order for (phallogocentric) civil-ization to happen.

Without the dichotomy of self/other, all other dichotomies would start to fall apart, Cixous says; her 'other bisexuality' would thus become a deconstructive force to erase the slashes in all structuring binary oppositions. When this occurs, the Western cultural repre-sentations of female sexuality – the myths associated with woman-hood – would also fall apart. Cixous focuses particularly on the myth of the Medusa, the woman with snakes for hair, whose look turns men into stone, and the myth of woman as black hole or abyss. The idea of woman as abyss is pretty easy to understand; in Freudian terms, a woman lacks a penis (positive, presence) and instead has this scary hole in which the penis disappears, and might not come back. Freud reads the Medusa myth as part of the fear of castration, the woman whose hair is writhing with lots of penises; she's scary, not because she has no penis, but because she has too many. Cixous says those are the fears that scare men into being complicit in upholding the phallogocentric order: they're scared of losing their one penis when they see women as having either no penis (and a black hole) or too many penises. Nowhere in these myths is there a depiction of the female body in itself, without reference to the penis. If women could show men their true sexual pleasures, their real bodies, by writing them in non-representational form, in *l'ecriture feminine*, Cixous says, men would understand that female bodies, female sexuality, is not about penises at all. That's why she says we have to show them our 'sexts' – another neologism, the combination of sex and texts, the idea of female sexuality as a new form of writing.

Cixous talks about hysterics as prior examples of women who write 'sexts,' who write their bodies as texts of *l'ecriture feminine*. Again she's following Freud, whose earliest works were on female hysterics. The basic idea of hysteria, for Freud, is that a body produces a symptom, such as the paralysis of a limb, which represents a repressed idea; the body thus 'speaks' what the conscious mind cannot say, and the unconscious thoughts are written out by the body itself. *L'ecriture feminine* has a lot in common with hysteria, as you can see, in the idea of the direct connections between the unconscious and the body as a mode of 'writing.'

Cixous concludes 'The Laugh of the Medusa' by offering a critique of the Freudian nuclear family, the mother–father–baby formation, which she sees as generating the ideas of castration and lack which form the basis for ideas of the feminine in both Freudian and Lacanian psychoanalysis. She wants to break up these 'old circuits' so that the family formations which uphold the phallogocentric Symbolic won't be re-created every time a child is born. She argues that this family system is just as limiting and oppressive to men as to women, and that it needs to be 'demater-paternalized.'[6] Then she discusses other ways to figure pregnancy, arguing that, like all functions of the female body, pregnancy needs to be written in *l'ecriture feminine*. When pregnancy is written this way, birth can be figured as something other than as separation or as lack.

She ends with the idea of formulating desire as a desire for everything, not for something lacking or absent, as in the Lacanian

Symbolic Order. Such a new desire would strip the penis of its significance as the signifier of lack, or of fulfillment of lack, and would free people to see each other as different beings, each of whom is whole, and who are not complementary, defined by difference or tied together in a binary opposition.

## LUCE IRIGARAY AND 'THIS SEX WHICH IS NOT ONE'

Luce Irigaray, like Hélène Cixous, follows the thinking of post-structuralist theorists in asking questions about the relationship between language and bodies, specifically male and female bodies and masculine and feminine language. Like Cixous, she focuses on the female body and how it has been constructed in phallogocentric systems like Freudian and Lacanian psychoanalysis. Irigaray, however, discusses the question of a female or feminine sexuality in more depth than Cixous; she wants specifically to explore the question of a feminine *jouissance* and what that might be when defined on its own terms, in reference to the female body only.

'Female sexuality has always been conceptualized on the basis of masculine parameters,' Irigaray declares in the first sentence of her essay 'This Sex Which Is Not One.' She's following Freud here, who defined all active erotic behavior as masculine, and all passive behavior as feminine; he also labeled clitoral sexual pleasure as active and masculine, and vaginal sexual pleasure as passive and feminine. Freud declared that the clitoris was literally a 'little penis,' insofar as it provided a masculine/phallic pleasure for women. Irigaray points out that, using Freud's definitions, female sexual organs and female eroticism are defined only in terms of male sex organs and male eroticism. If the female sex organ is the clitoris, then it is really a penis, and one smaller and less powerful than the male version; if the female sex organ is the vagina, then it is passive, waiting to be filled with a penis.

Note the 'if's in the above statements: if the female sex organ is the clitoris, if the female sex organ is the vagina. This, for Irigaray, is a central flaw in psychoanalytic theory and in Western cultural thought: we don't know how to talk about female sexuality, and female bodily configurations, because we are focused on finding the *one* female sexual organ. Irigaray points out that Freud has 'nothing to say' about woman and her sexual pleasure: 'nothing' because Freudian psychoanalysis defines female pleasure solely in terms of male bodies, and 'nothing' because Freud defines female genitalia as 'nothing,' since there is 'nothing' to see, 'nothing' visibly present, in the supposedly already-castrated female.

Freudian psychoanalysis insists on each sex having only one visible and nameable sex organ, based on Freud's notion that the penis is the only male sex organ; in so doing, he claims women have no sex organ, and also ignores all the other parts, such as testicles, that are part of the male body. Irigaray asks why Freud, and Western culture in general, needs to have just sex organ for each sex. Is it because we need to have a single word, a unique signifier, to represent sexuality in one specific locus on the body? Irigaray here is questioning the basic structure of Western metaphysics, the binary opposition, which requires that there be one signifier, and only one, on each side of the slash.

For male sexuality, this has been relatively unproblematic, as Freud and Lacan both agree that 'penis' is the signifier for male sexuality, the left side of the slash. But if 'penis' is one side of a binary opposition, what's on the other side? Look at some of the possibilities:

- Penis/vagina
- Penis/clitoris
- Penis/no penis
- Penis/nothing

All of these definitions (and perhaps more) appear in psychoanalytic attempts to name *the* female sexual organ that is the counterpart of the penis. For poststructuralist feminists such as Irigaray, this list is inherently deconstructive: if you can't find one term, and one term only, to be on the right side of the slash, the opposite of 'penis,' then the whole system of binary oppositions, the phallogocentric system of Western metaphysics, starts to fall apart.

Female sexual pleasure, or *jouissance*, according to Irigaray, is of a different order, in a different economy than male sexual pleasure, because the male and female bodies are configured so differently. Man needs an instrument with which to touch himself, she argues; if his pleasure is indeed based in his penis, then something else – a hand, a vagina, a mouth, language – has to touch the penis in order to produce pleasure. The female sexual organs – and Irigaray insists that they are plural – are, by contrast, always in contact with each other; the layers of labia enfold the clitoris and provide constant autoerotic contact. Thus female sexual pleasure needs no external object, but is complete unto itself.

From this, Irigaray posits heterosexual intercourse as a 'violation,' an interruption of female autoerotic pleasure, as the penis forces apart the labia and forces female sexuality back into a phallic order. She calls this a form of 'rape,' naming heterosexual intercourse as 'foreign to the feminine.'

Irigaray links the male desire for intercourse with the desire to return to the original union with the mother's body, which is forbidden in both Freud and Lacan's accounts of human development. In intercourse, then, the female partner's body is only a 'prop' for a male fantasy of reunion and re-merging. The female partner's desire – which, presumably, is the same as the male's desire, that is, to return to and merge with the maternal body – has no place in heterosexual intercourse, according to this model; the woman can't fantasize that she's joining with the mother's body when the man is having that fantasy while joining with her body. In fact, Irigaray claims, the man's pursuit of his own desire to merge with the mother's body, expressed as vaginal intercourse, actively interrupts the woman's communion with her own autoeroticism, with her labia constantly touching each other.

Irigaray is advocating for masturbation or lesbian sexual activity as the only means for female desire to be expressed in female terms. She argues that feminine desire, so long molded by and into masculine parameters, is like a 'lost civilization,' one which has a 'different alphabet' and a 'different language.' This lost desire, lost civilization, lost language was 'submerged by the logic which has dominated the West since the Greeks.' This logic is what Derrida discusses as logocentrism and Cixous names phallogocentrism: the preference for presence over absence, for things that are visible over things that are invisible, for things that have a definite and singular shape or form over things that have an ambiguous or fluid shape or form. Freudian and Lacanian psychoanalytic constructions of male and female sexual desire follow this logic, according to Irigaray, preferring the visible bounded penis to the hidden and amorphous female genitalia, which become 'nothing to see.'

Irigaray points out how dependent the phallogocentric Symbolic Order is on the register of the visible, as Lacan requires that entry into the Symbolic be preceded by the misrecognition of one's self in the mirror stage as a visual experience. The Western emphasis on vision, which marks female genitalia as 'nothing to see,' subsumes all other sensory registers to that of vision. Touch thus belongs to the realm of the repressed, the unconscious, the realm of the maternal body and the Real which must be abandoned in order to enter the specular Symbolic Order. For Irigaray, the primary form of female desire, of female eroticism based solely on the configuration of the female body, lies in touch, not in sight, and hence female desire does not require the unity and phallomorphism which the visual dimensions of phallogocentrism demand.

Women's pleasure, their *jouissance*, comes from touch, and from the idea that woman is constantly touching herself because her 'sex,' her genitalia, are not singular but multiple. Similarly, according to Irigaray, female language – Cixous's *l'ecriture feminine* – is equally multiple and amorphous, rather than single and linear, like the penis (in psychoanalytic thought). The female body can speak from everywhere, in Irigaray's view, because the female body experiences pleasure everywhere. Like Cixous, Irigaray does not try to define or categorize this language of female erotic pleasure, noting instead that it is inherently slippery, unfixed, fluid, and doesn't make 'sense' in the way that traditional phallogocentric language does.

Irigaray's critique of the phallogocentric Symbolic Order is more radical that Cixous's critique, if only because Irigaray rejects heterosexuality as irredeemably patriarchal. She argues, in this essay and elsewhere, that the articulation and celebration of lesbian sexuality will work as a deconstructive force, shaking the foundations of patriarchal phallogocentric systems of meaning and exchange. The radical potential of non-heterosexual forms of writing and desire is an important part of queer theory, the topic of the next chapter.

## NOTES

1 Sandra Gilbert and Susan Gubar, *The Madwoman in the Attic: The Woman Writer and the Nineteenth Century Literary Imagination*. New Haven, CT: Yale University Press, 1979, p. 3.
2 *Ibid.*, p. 7.
3 Hélène Cixous, 'The Laugh of the Medusa,' in Hazard Adams and Leroy Searle, eds, *Critical Theory Since 1965*. Gainesville, FL: University Press of Florida, 1986, p. 310.
4 *Ibid.*, p. 319.
5 *Ibid.*, p. 314.
6 *Ibid.*, pp. 318–19.

## SUGGESTIONS FOR FURTHER READING

Sarah Gamble, *The Routledge Companion to Feminism and Postfeminism*. New York: Routledge, 2002.

Toril Moi, *Sexual/Textual Politics: Feminist Literary Theory*. New York: Routledge, 2002

Linda Nicholson, *The Second Wave: A Reader in Feminist Theory*. New York: Routledge, 1997.

Susan Alice Watkins, *Introducing Feminism*. New York: Totem Books, 2001.

Chris Weedon, *Feminist Practice and Poststructuralist Theory*. Oxford: Blackwell, 1996.

# CHAPTER 7

# QUEER THEORY

Let's start by listing all the associations you might have with the word 'queer.' What does 'queer' make you think of.

Chances are, you listed words like 'homosexual,' 'odd,' 'gay,' and the like. The word 'queer' in queer theory has some of these connotations, particularly its alignment with ideas about homosexuality. Queer theory is a relatively new branch of study or theoretical speculation; it has only been named as an area since about 1991. It grew out of gay/lesbian studies, a discipline which itself is very new, existing in any kind of organized form only since about the mid-1980s. Gay/lesbian studies, in turn, grew out of feminist studies and feminist theory.

Feminist theory, in the mid- to late 1970s, looked at gender as a system of signs, or signifiers, assigned to sexually dimorphic bodies, which served to differentiate the social roles and meanings those bodies could have. Feminist theory thus argued that gender was a social construct, something designed and implemented and perpetuated by social organizations and structures, rather than something merely 'true,' something innate to the ways bodies worked on a biological level. In so doing, feminist theory made two very important contributions. The first is that feminist theory separated the social from the biological, insisting that we see a difference between what is the product of human ideas, hence something mutable and changeable, and what is the product of biology, hence something (relatively) stable and unchangeable. The second contribution is related to the first: by separating the social and the biological, the constructed and the innate, feminist theory insisted that gender was not something 'essential' to an individual's identity.

This word 'essential' is important in theories which tell us about how individual identities are constructed within social organizations.

The humanist idea of identity, or self, focuses on the notion that your identity is unique to you, that who you are is the product of some core self, some unchangeable aspects or markers that are at the heart and center of 'you.' These aspects usually include sex (I am male or female), gender (I am masculine or feminine), sexuality (I am heterosexual or homosexual), religious beliefs (I am Christian, Jewish, Buddhist), and nationality (I am American, Russian, Vietnamese). Within humanist thought, these core aspects of identity are considered to be 'essences,' things that are unchangeable and unchanging, things that make you who you are under all circumstances, no matter what happens to you. This concept of an essential self separates 'self' from everything outside of self – not just 'other,' but also all historical events, all things that do change and shift. You might think of the humanist notion of essential selfhood in survivalist terms: the self exists inside an armored shelter, where nothing that happens in the outside world can touch it. The self might feel jarred or shaken by explosions in the outside world, which rattle the doors of the shelter, but it cannot be substantially changed by what happens outside. It can, however, be destroyed. But those are the only options – the essential self can exist in an unchanging state or be wiped out, but nothing in between.

Feminist theory, by challenging the idea that gender is part of this essential self, caused a 'rupture,' a break, that revealed the constructedness of this supposedly natural self. Feminist theory wasn't alone in causing this rupture; similar kinds of breaks occurred within theories of race and national identity, among others, which contributed to the 'deconstruction' of the idea of the essential self. From this rupture came the poststructuralist idea of selfhood as a constructed idea, something not 'naturally' produced by bodies or by birth. Selfhood, in poststructuralist theory, becomes 'subjecthood' or 'subjectivity.' The switch in terms is a recognition that, first of all, human identity is shaped by language, by becoming a subject in language (as we saw with Lacan et al.). The shift from 'self' to 'subject' also marks the idea that subjects are the product of signs, or signifiers, which make up our ideas of identity. Selves are stable and essential; subjects are constructed, hence provisional, shifting, changing, always able to be redefined or reconstructed. Selves, in this sense, are like signifiers within a rigid system, whose meanings are fixed; subjects, by contrast, are like signifiers in a system with more play, more multiplicity of meaning.

Once feminist theory had helped to rupture the humanist idea of stable or essential selfhood, and specifically the idea of stable or essential gender identity, and replaced it with the poststructuralist idea of gender identity as a set of shifting signifiers, other forms of theory began to question other 'essentialist' notions of identity. As we will see, ideas of race as innate, essential, or biological came under scrutiny (particularly within feminism, as the idea of the female subject posited in feminist theory in the 1970s was uniformly white and middle-class). Similarly, ideas about sexuality as an innate or essentialist category also became open to reformulation. This is where gay/lesbian studies, as a discipline and as the academic arm of a political movement, began, in the early to mid-1980s.

## FLEXIBLE SEXUALITY?

It is, perhaps, more difficult than with gender to see sexuality as socially constructed, rather than as biological. When we look around, we see 'gender bending' happening in lots of arenas – movies like *The Birdcage* and *Boys Don't Cry*, to name only two, bend the idea of gender roles as essential, and as determined by sex (males are masculine, females are feminine). In fact, we can see gender roles and gender signifiers shifting daily: how many women, ten years ago, had visible tattoos, for instance, and how many men would sport visible piercings, in ears or other body parts? Thinking of these changes (and you can come up with your own examples of flexible or shifting gender constructs), it's relatively easy to see gender as a system of signifiers.

Sexuality is harder, though, in part because of the way our culture has always taught us to think about sexuality. While gender may be a matter of style of dress, sexuality seems to be about biology, about how bodies operate on a basic level. Our culture tends to define sexuality in two ways: in terms of animal instincts, of behaviors programmed by hormones or by seasonal cycles, over which our free will has no control, and in terms of moral and ethical choices, of behaviors that are coded as either good or evil, moral or immoral, and over which we are supposed to have complete (or almost complete) rigid control. In the first way of thinking about sexuality, sexual responses are almost purely biological: we respond sexually to what is coded in our genes and hormones, and this is almost always defined in terms of reproductive behavior. This viewpoint comes from evolutionary thought, where it is the duty of each member of the species to try to preserve and pass on her or his particular genetic make-up. This view says we can understand human sexual behavior by understanding animal sexual behavior.

The problem with this first view is that human sexuality doesn't work like animal sexuality. If it did, all the females would come into heat at certain cycles, and all the males would frantically try to have sex with them during these cycles; all sexual activity would be geared toward reproduction, and sexual activity in both sexes would occur only during these periods of heat. Obviously, human sexuality works differently. In fact, human sexuality looks very little like animal sexuality in any regard. We are (with perhaps the exception of the bonobo ape) the only species that can copulate more or less at will, without regard to fertility or hormonal cycles, and that alone separates sexual behavior from reproduction for human beings. We also have an enormous repertoire of sexual behaviors and activities, only some of which are linked to reproduction, which further separates the two categories. And – most importantly – human sexual behavior is about pleasure, and about pleasure mediated by all kinds of cultural categories.

Yes, we could argue about forms of animal sexuality and how they do or do not model human sexuality – I have a spayed female dog who likes to 'hump' people's legs, which is an example of sexual behavior not linked to reproductive activity – but the point is that linking human sexuality to animal sexuality serves to construct sexuality in particular ways. If you see humans largely as animals, then you also see human sexuality as largely reproductive in nature, in essence – and thus any behavior not linked to reproduction becomes 'unnatural.' Which leads us to the second way our culture defines sexuality: in terms of morality, in terms of right and wrong behaviors.

Western cultural ideas about sexuality come from lots of places – from science (and particularly from the evolutionary view of sexuality as an animalistic instinctive behavior), from religion, from politics, and from economics, for example. These categories of sexual codification are investigated by Michel Foucault in his series entitled *The History of Sexuality*. Examples of sexuality being defined by politics and economics occur when nations or other social organizations worry about population control, and urge people not to reproduce – or even require abortions or birth control or sterilization to ensure that; a counter-example of sexuality defined by politics and economics would be in countries or subgroups who urge members to produce lots of children, so that that group will have a greater population than some other group.

These ideas about sexuality often take the form of moral statements about what forms of sexuality are right, or good, or moral, and which are wrong, bad, and immoral. These categories have shifted over time, which is another way of arguing that definitions of sexuality are not 'essential' or timeless or innate, but rather are social constructs, things that can change and be manipulated. Certainly we've seen such changes in the past ten years, not just in relation to homosexuality and heterosexuality, but in relation to ideas of safe sex and the prevention of sexually transmitted disease: in today's culture (in some circles), an immoral sex act might be one that doesn't include a condom or other form of barrier, rather than one that merely isn't involved in a reproductive activity. In previous generations, as in current times, these ways of defining sexuality (through biology, religion, politics, and economics) have produced clear-cut categories of what is right and wrong, usually categories linked to ideas about reproduction and family life. Queer activist Gayle Rubin's article 'Thinking Sex: Notes for a Radical Theory of the Politics of Sexuality' argues that ideas about sexuality are structured in binary oppositions, where one side of the pair is positive, good, moral, right, and the other side is negative, bad, immoral, and wrong.

Rubin argues for the deconstruction of all these binary oppositions; she is, in fact, arguing for the complete separation of all forms of sexual behavior from any kind of moral judgment. And this is where lots of people have a hard time agreeing with her (or with other sexuality radicals). Doesn't it seem that some kinds of sexual behavior *should* be wrong? What about sex that hurts someone else, sex that is not consensual, sex between someone with lots of power and someone with no power? These objections show two things: one is that sexual behavior, in human culture, is almost always about something more than just pleasure and/or reproduction: it's often about forms of power and dominance. The other thing these objections show is how powerful the links are between sexual activities and notions of morality. And the link comes, in part, from defining sexuality as part of *identity*, rather than just as an activity which one might engage in. Hence, if you have genital sexual contact with someone of the same sex, you are not just having homosexual sex, you are a homosexual. And that identity is then linked to a moral judgment about both homosexual acts and homosexual identities. The recent movie *Brokeback Mountain* illustrates how powerful these ideas have been – and to some extent still are – in Western (both Anglo-European and US Western) culture.

## GAY/LESBIAN STUDIES

Gay/lesbian studies looks at the kinds of social structures and social constructs which define our ideas about sexuality as act and sexuality as identity. As an academic field, gay/lesbian studies looks at how notions of homosexuality have historically been defined – and of course, in doing so, also look at how its binary opposite, heterosexuality, has been defined. Gay/lesbian studies also looks at how various cultures, or various time periods, have enforced ideas about what kinds of sexuality are normal and which are abnormal, which are moral and which are immoral.

Gay/lesbian literary criticism, a subset of gay/lesbian studies, looks at images of sexuality, and ideas of normative and deviant behavior, in a number of ways: by finding gay/lesbian authors whose sexuality has been masked or erased in history and biography; by looking at texts by gay/lesbian authors to discover particular literary themes, techniques, and perspectives which come from being a homosexual in a heterosexual world; by looking at texts – by gay or straight authors – which depict homosexuality and heterosexuality, or which focus on sexuality as a constructed (rather than essential) concept; and by looking at how literary texts (by gay or straight authors) operate in conjunction with non-literary texts to provide a culture with ways to think about sexuality.

Gay/lesbian studies, as a political form of academics, also challenges the notion of normative sexualities. As the prevalence of the structure of the binary opposition tells us, once you set up a category labeled 'normal,' you automatically set up its opposite, a category labeled 'deviant,' and the specific acts or identities which fill those categories then get linked to other forms of social practices and methods of social control. When you do something your culture labels deviant, you are liable to be punished for it: by being arrested, by being shamed, made to feel dirty, by losing your job, your license, your loved ones, your self-respect, your health insurance. Gay/lesbian studies, like feminist studies, works to understand how these categories of normal and deviant are constructed, how they operate, how they are enforced, in order to intervene into changing or ending them.

Which brings me – finally – to queer theory. Queer theory emerges from gay/lesbian studies' attention to the social construction of categories of normative and deviant sexual behavior. But while gay/lesbian studies, as the name implies, focused largely on questions of homosexuality, queer theory expands its realm of investigation. Queer theory looks at, and studies, and has a political critique of, anything that falls into normative and deviant categories, particularly sexual activities and identities. The word 'queer,' as it appears in the dictionary, has a primary meaning of 'odd,' 'peculiar,' 'out of the ordinary.' Queer theory concerns itself with any and all forms of sexuality that are 'queer' in this sense – and then, by extension, with the normative behaviors and identities which define what is 'queer' (by being their binary opposites). Thus queer theory expands the scope of its analysis to all kinds of behaviors, including those which are gender-bending as well as those which involve 'queer' non-normative forms of sexuality.

Queer theory insists that all sexual behaviors, all concepts linking sexual behaviors to sexual identities, and all categories of normative and deviant sexualities, are social constructs, sets of signifiers which create certain types of social meaning. Queer theory follows feminist theory and gay/lesbian studies in rejecting the idea that sexuality is an essentialist category, something determined by biology or judged by eternal standards of morality and truth. For queer theorists, sexuality is a complex array of social codes and forces, forms of individual activity and institutional power, which interact to shape the ideas of what is normative and what is deviant at any particular moment, and which then operate under the rubric of what is 'natural,' 'essential,' 'biological,' or 'god-given.'

One of the most important contemporary queer theorists is Judith Butler, whose work on *Gender Trouble* uses concepts from Freudian psychoanalysis to question cultural assumptions about gender and sexuality. 'Bricolage' is perhaps the best term to use to think about what Judith Butler does to and with Freud's psychoanalysis. She uses bits and pieces of Freud in order to problematize gender and sexuality as categories of essence. She wants to question the idea that a person *is* male or female, masculine or feminine, which are the fundamental ideas Freud started with. Butler wants to show that gender is not simply a social construct, but rather a kind of performance, a show we put on, a set of signs we wear, as costume or disguise – hence as far from essence as can be.

She starts by asking questions about the category 'woman:' who does it include, and how do we know who it includes? And who decides what's in this category anyway? We've already gone over this: in phallogocentric Western discourse, 'woman' is always the other of 'man,' hence excluded from culture or the Symbolic. In feminist theory, 'woman' is a universal category, which thus excludes ideas of differences among women (differences of race, class, or sexuality, for example). Both types of theory – psychoanalytic and feminist – rely on a notion of 'woman' as referring to an essence, a fact, a biological given, hence a universal.

Butler says we need to think about 'woman' as multiple and discontinuous, not as a category with 'ontological integrity.' She turns to psychoanalytic theory to do so.[1] She gives an overview of Freud and Lacan as setting up 'woman' as an eternal abstract universal category, and implicates Irigaray in doing the same thing. Then she points to the poststructuralist theoretical feminists who destabilize the concept of the subject as masculine/male by saying that the female isn't a subject, isn't fully in the Symbolic, that 'woman' is on the margins, in the body, and is thus more free to play than man. But, if 'woman' is not a subject, can she have agency? And if there is no normative or unitary concept of 'woman,' can we have feminism as a movement or as a theory? If there's no single 'woman,' then there can be no single feminism.

Thus the problem is to think about 'woman' as fragmentations, and about feminism without a single unitary concept of 'woman.' Butler then looks at how psychoanalysis constructs 'woman' as a unitary category. Psychoanalysis is a story about origins and ends, which includes some aspects, and excludes others. The story starts with a utopian non-differentiation of the sexes, which is ended by enforced separation and the creation of difference. This narrative 'gives a false sense of legitimacy and universality to a culturally specific and, in some cases, culturally oppressive version of gender identity.'[2]

In a way, Butler is asking the question about what happens in a psychoanalytic paradigm if you don't have a mother and father and no one else; if you're raised by a single parent, or two parents of the same sex, or by a grandmother, or by a TV set or computer. She looks at how Freud's versions of the Oedipus Complex privilege a certain story, a certain pattern of identifications, that supposedly produce a coherent unified gendered self (man, woman, masculine, feminine), and says no, that's not how it really works – you could have variations, fragmented identities, discontinuous or provisional understandings of our gender identities based on a wider variety of identifications, beyond just mother/father/child.

Freud sets up a system where certain identifications are primary in forming a (gendered) self, and others are secondary; the primary identifications have more power to shape a self than the secondary ones, and are subordinated/subsumed within the primary ones. Hence relations with the mother are primary (for both sexes), while relations with siblings, for example, are secondary, not as important in the narrative of how the gendered self is formed. The primary/secondary identifications are temporal: the primary ones happen first, the secondary are added on. Without that temporal placement (first this happens, then this happens), you couldn't tell which identifications were more important than others – which were substance and which were attributes. If we could redesign the Oedipal narrative so it that wasn't linear/temporal, we'd have all the identifications going on at once, or without ranking – so that all would be equally important, all would be attributes without one being substance (or all would be copies without one being original).

Butler wants to understand gendered subjectivity 'as a history of identifications, parts of which can be brought into play in given contexts and which, precisely because they encode the contingencies of personal history, do not always point back to an internal coherence of any kind.'[3]

She then presents the idea that the concept of the unconscious makes any idea of coherence or unity suspect – whether we're talking about a slip of the tongue, or any narrative/story – including the Oedipal story of psychoanalysis. Freud's story works hard to be unitary and coherent, to tell a connected story about how gender is formed. It does so by repressing certain elements, excluding them from the story. One of the ways it achieves this is to repress or exclude ideas of simultaneity and multiplicity in gender and sexual identity. According to Freud, you either identify with a sex or you desire it; only those two relations are possible. Thus it's not possible to desire the sex you identify with. If you are a man desiring another man, for instance, Freud would say that's because you 'really' identify with women.

LITERARY THEORY: A GUIDE FOR THE PERPLEXED

Butler looks at how Freud tells the story of how fantasy identifications (identifications that happen in the unconscious) shape our
identity (who we are). When we identify with someone else, we create
an internal image of that person, or, more precisely, who we want
that person to be, and then we identify with that internalized and
idealized image. Our own identity, then, isn't modeled on actual
others but on our image of their image, on what we want the other
to be, rather than what the other really is.

Gender, as the identification with one sex, or one object (like the
mother), is a fantasy, a set of internalized images, and not a set of
properties governed by the body and its organ configuration. Rather,
gender is a set of signs internalized, psychically imposed on the body
and on one's psychic sense of identity. Gender, Butler concludes,
is thus not a primary category, but an attribute, a set of secondary
narrative effects.

Gender is a fantasy enacted by 'corporeal styles that constitute
bodily significations.'[4] In other words, gender is an act, a performance, a set of manipulated codes, costumes, rather than a core aspect
of essential identity. Butler's main metaphor for this is 'drag,' i.e.
dressing like a person of the 'opposite sex.' All gender is a form of
'drag,' according to Butler; there is no 'real' core gender to refer to.

## NOTES

1 Judith Butler, 'Gender Trouble, Feminist Theory, and Psychoanalytic
  Discourse,' in Linda J. Nicholson, ed., *Feminism/Postmodernism*. New
  York and London: Routledge, 1990, p. 325.
2 *Ibid.*, p. 330.
3 *Ibid.*, p. 331.
4 *Ibid.*, p. 334.

## SUGGESTIONS FOR FURTHER READING

Henry Abelove, Michele Aina Berale, and David Halperin, eds, *The Lesbian
  and Gay Studies Reader*. New York: Routledge, 1993.
Judith Butler, *Undoing Gender*. New York: Taylor and Francis, 2004.
Annamarie Jagose, *Queer Theory: An Introduction*. New York: New York
  University Press, 1997.
Nikki Sullivan, *A Critical Introduction to Queer Theory*. New York: New
  York University Press, 1993.
Elizabeth Weed and Naomi Schor, eds, *Feminism Meets Queer Theory*.
  Bloomington, IN: Indiana University Press, 1997.

# INTERLUDE: HISTORY TO HISTORICISM

So far we've seen how language operates as structure, and how words, or signs, have meaning, we've also seen how binary oppositions create the basic structures through which we are taught to think about our world, and how we can begin to undo, or deconstruct, some of those ways of thinking. We've seen how a human infant becomes a speaking subject, taking up a position within the structure of language, and how gender and sexuality are shaped and limited by the subject positions available within a fixed system. We've heard about alternative forms of language, where meaning is more fluid and the structure less rigid, and we've been told that these 'feminine' modes of meaning can be deconstructive, shaking up the binary oppositions and the linguistic structures which shape, which *are*, our reality.

What we haven't looked at is what people actually think, and do, and say, and write, in the world we inhabit; we haven't looked directly at the *content* of any of these systems or subject positions. We haven't talked about what a subject might believe or say from a particular subject position. We haven't talked about how these deconstructive forces that rattle binary structures might *change* those structures, or what would happen if we succeeded in putting more play into our language and into our belief systems. We haven't talked about any of the mechanisms a specific society might use to try to keep its subjects in their 'proper' positions – in their seats, if you will – or how subjects might resist their assigned positions. And we still haven't talked much, if at all, about what any of these theories have to do with *literature*.

The next chapters will examine these ideas. We'll look at *ideology* to understand how individual subjects come to believe the things they believe, and how they act on those beliefs. We'll look at what people actually do with language by examining *discourse* (including literature!), the bodies of writing that cultures produce to organize, preserve, and distribute knowledge. We'll also look more closely at the interrelations of ideologies and discourses, and about strategies by which subjects can uphold, alter, and resist the positions and ideas their cultures offer.

The theories of ideology and discourse covered in Chapter 8 come from a variety of disciplines or perspectives, including Marxism, cultural anthropology, psychology, and linguistics. They all share certain assumptions and premises, however, as all have been developed within the framework of structuralist and poststructuralist ideas about the mind, the world, and the relations between the two. The theories covered in Chapter 8 may be said to belong generally to a school of thought, or mode of analysis, called 'New Historicism.' So before we launch into the specifics of the theories of ideology and discourse, let's take a moment to understand the basic ideas of New Historicist analysis.

## HUMANIST HISTORY

It has never been quite clear, within the structure of the university, whether departments of history belong to the Humanities or the Social Sciences. Like scientists, historians are supposed to be objective scholars in search of accurate verifiable facts which demonstrate patterns of cause and effect that occur in a linear pattern. Like scientists, they search for 'the truth' of historical events in order to tell them from a single objective perspective or point of view. But, like humanists, historians are also in search of historical events and periods that point to universal human truths and transcendent values of what is true and good; like literary critics, they read historical texts to uncover the 'spirit of the age' and present representative individuals whose life and works embody that 'spirit.'

This kind of history has had a mixed relationship with literary studies. History can tell literary critics useful facts about an author's biography, or the 'spirit' of the time in which a particular work was written. New Criticism, however, which was the dominant critical method in literary studies from the 1930s to the 1960s, had little use for historical contexts, insisting that meaning came completely from the literary text itself, without reference to any external factors, such as the cultural milieu in which the author, text, and readers lived.

With the advent of structuralist and poststructuralist paradigms for thinking about how people make meaning in their worlds, however, the assumptions and methodologies of history changed – along with those of literary studies, anthropology, sociology, psychology, linguistics, and lots of other academic disciplines. Discarding the humanist beliefs in objective analysis, linear sequences of causal relations, the inevitability of progress, and the idea of the 'spirit of the age,' historians began to ask different kinds of questions and to look at different kinds of materials to make different kinds of assessments. The result has been named 'New Historicism,' which is best defined as a set of assumptions shared by history, anthropology, literary studies, and the social sciences in general.

My own encounter with the distinction between the old history and the new historicism occurred when I was writing my doctoral disseration in graduate school. I was working with professors in the English department and with a professor in the history department, examining cultural texts from the last two decades of nineteenth-century US middle-class culture to see how they constructed ideas of gender and disability. In one of the many meetings I had with my history professor to discuss drafts of my dissertation chapters, she pointed to a particular passage I'd written and commented, 'Mary, you are making this up.' I replied as an English major: 'Of course I am. It's my interpretation.' My professor, trained in the 'old' methods of history, wanted me to find factual evidence to prove that the statements and conclusions I was making were in fact true. With my training in literary analysis, I saw nothing wrong with using the source I cited as if it were open to interpretation and offering my particular reading of it.

## NEW HISTORICISM

New Historicism might best be described as a textual practice or set of strategies for reading, rather than as a unified theory or doctrine; you might recall that Derrida made a similar claim for deconstruction. With New Historicism – also called 'cultural poetics' or 'cultural criticism' – all texts are created equal: anything written, any piece of *discourse*, is treated as a piece of writing open to interpretation and analysis. New Historicism, as used in the disciplines of history, anthropology, and literary studies, starts with the assumption that history is a story a culture tells itself about its past, rather than a set of provable facts. New Historicism examines texts as narratives, using many of the same assumptions and techniques developed in (pre- and poststructuralist) literary analysis, including an examination of the narrator's point of view, the author's social position, influences, and motivations, the rhetorical devices employed (or left out), and the implied audience the writing is meant to persuade. New Historicism also assumes that any text can be deconstructed to reveal its own ideological assumptions, contradictions, and limitations.

New Historicism, or poststructuralist cultural studies, takes as its object of study any cultural 'text,' broadly defined, including written documents, rituals, performances, speeches, advertisements, and any form of cultural practice that makes meaning within the culture. New Historicism as a strategy for analyzing cultural meaning draws on the work of anthropologist Clifford Geertz, who took from Claude Levi-Strauss the idea that 'culture' is a system of signs or codes that govern behavior of individuals, groups, and institutions. Unlike Levi-Strauss, Geertz is not a structuralist, and is not interested in the *langue* of a culture, or in finding elements within a structure which are cultural universals. Rather, Geertz calls attention to the individual *paroles* within a cultural signifying system; these *paroles* can be any event, small or large, that contains and conveys some kind of cultural meaning. Geertz uses a method he calls 'thick description,' which is similar to the practice of 'close reading' fundamental to all textual interpretation in literary studies; only by noting every possible detail of the activity or practice being analyzed, Geertz argues, can one begin to piece together the layers of meaning that the practice has for the person or people performing it.

The theories of Louis Althusser, Mikhail Bakhtin, and Michel Foucault, which are discussed in Chapter 8, all participate in these principles of New Historicism. All are interested in how a subject within a culture makes meaning and acts in accordance with the meanings he or she understands. All share the idea that individual identity is shaped by countless external cultural influences, the discourses which make available the meanings for each action, event, or idea that occurs within a culture. Most believe that individual belief and cultural discourse are also mutually constitutive – that they influence and shape each other, rather than the cultural discourse providing the only framework for interpretation and meaning. All assume that every expressive act is always part of a network of material practices, and that every belief or idea exists in the mind and in the behavior of the individuals which hold them. All, in short, are interested in what a subject believes and how he or she acts within a cultural context to make meaning out of the world and its events. All discard the notion of history as 'what happened' in favor of the new historicist concern with how cultural *meaning* emerges from historical events.

# CHAPTER 8

# IDEOLOGY AND DISCOURSE

The title 'Ideology and Discourse' refers to the ideas that link the three main theories and theorists this chapter addresses. Louis Althusser, Mikhail Bakhtin, and Michel Foucault are all are discussing how ideology works, and how ideologies construct subjects. All of these theorists are coming from a Marxist perspective, using ideas and terms developed in Marxist theory. So, to start off, I want to talk a bit about some of the fundamental premises of Marxist theory.

## MARXIST THEORY: A FEW BASICS

Marxism is a set of theories, or a system of thought and analysis, developed by Karl Marx in the nineteenth century in response to the Western industrial revolution and the rise of industrial capitalism as the predominant economic mode. Like feminist theory and queer theory, Marxist theory is directed at social change; Marxists want to analyze social relations in order to change them, in order to alter what they see are the gross injustices and inequalities created by capitalist economic relations. My capsule summary of the main ideas of Marxism, however, will focus on the theoretical aspects more than on how that theory has been and is applicable to projects for social change.

Marxist theory is fundamentally a historical materialist view of the world; it combines elements of philosophy, history, and economic theory to assert the premise that our world and our history are products of how human beings use tools to create the material culture we live in. All social organizations and forces, and all social change or 'history,' is determined ultimately by the work that people do with their tools. These tools are often referred to as 'instruments of production,' or as 'forces of production.' Historical materialism also says that people and the tools they use always exist in some sort of social relations, because people live in social groups, not in isolation, and they always organize their social groups in some way, such as having a form of 'government.' What every social group organizes, according to the historical materialist perspective, is how people work with their tools, or, in other words, how human labor, and forces of production, operate. The organizations that shape how people use the forces of production are called the 'relations of production.' The relations of production, how people relate to each other, and to their society as a whole, through their productive activity, and the forces of production together form what historical materialism calls a *mode of production*.

As an economic theory, Marxism looks specifically at the capitalist economic system, based on an analysis of how the forces and relations of production work within the capitalist mode of production. In a factory, for instance, a worker performs labor on raw materials, and thus transforms those raw materials into an object; in the process, the laborer adds something to the raw materials so that the object (raw material + labor) is worth more than the original raw material. What the laborer adds is called 'surplus value,' in Marxist theory. While the laborer is paid for the work he or she does, that payment is figured in terms of 'reproduction,' of what the laborer will need in order to come back the next day (i.e. food, rest, shelter, clothes, etc.), and not in terms of what value the laborer added to the raw material. The goal of capitalist production is to sell the object made, with its surplus value, for more than the cost of the raw materials and the reproduction of the laborer. This excess in value (in price) comes from the surplus value added by the laborer, but it is 'owned' by the capitalist; the factory owner gets the profit from selling the object, and the laborer gets only the cost of his 'reproduction' in the wages he earns.

From these economic relations comes a crucially important concept in Marxist thought: the idea of *alienation*. There are two aspects to the Marxist idea of alienation. The first is that labor which produces surplus value is alienated labor. The labor put into an object becomes part of the capitalist's profit, and thus no longer belongs to the laborer. In addition to alienating the laborer from his labor power, capitalism also forces the worker to become alienated from himself. When a worker has to sell his labor power, he becomes a *commodity*, something to be sold in the marketplace like a thing; the worker who is a commodity is thus not fully human, in the philosophical sense, since he cannot exercise free will to determine his actions. The worker who is forced to exist as a commodity in the labor market is alienated from his humanness; in selling one's labor, that labor becomes alienated, something separate from or other than the laborer, something divided from the person that produces it. The double alienation of the proletariat, and their exploitation by the capitalists, form the basic contradictions of capitalism which produce the dialectic (the struggle between workers and owners, labor and capital) which produces social change, or history, and which will eventually, according to Marxist theory, synthesize into socialism.

From Marx's economic doctrines comes an analysis of how the capitalist system specifically functions; from historical materialism comes a model of how social organizations are structured, which is relevant to all cultures, whether capitalist or not. According to the Marxist view of culture, the modes of production are the primary determining factor in all social relations: everything that happens in a society is in some way related to, and determined by, the mode of production or economic *base*.

The economic base in any society generates other social formations, called the *superstructure*. The superstructure consists of all other kinds of social activities or systems, including politics, religion, philosophy, morality, art, and science. All of these aspects of a society are, in Marxist theory, shaped, formed, or created by the economic base. Thus a central question for a lot of Marxist theory is *how* the economic base determines superstructure. How, for instance, does the feudal mode of production produce or determine the religious beliefs and practices current during the medieval period?

Another way of asking this question is to look at the relations between economic base and a particular aspect of superstructure, which Marxists name *ideology*. Ideology, or ideologies, are the ideas that exist in a culture; there will typically be one or several kinds of religious ideologies, for example, and political ideologies, and aesthetic ideologies, which will articulate what, and how, people can think about religion, politics, and art, respectively. Ideology is how a society thinks about itself, the forms of social consciousness that exist at any particular moment; ideologies supply all the terms and assumptions and frameworks that individuals use to understand their culture, and ideologies supply all the things that people believe in, and then act on.

For Marx, ideology, as part of the superstructure generated by an economic base, works to justify that base; the ideologies present in a capitalist society will explain, justify, and support the capitalist mode of production. In nineteenth-century southern US culture, for example, the economic base was slave labor, and all of the super-structures, such as organized religion, local and national politics, and art (especially literature), worked to uphold slavery as a good economic system.

Literature, then, is part of any culture's superstructure, from this perspective, and is determined, in both form and content, by the economic base. Literature also participates in the articulation of forms of cultural ideology – novels and poems might justify or attack religious beliefs, political beliefs, or aesthetic ideas. Marxist literary critics and theorists are interested in asking a range of questions about how literature functions as a site for ideology, as part of the superstructure. First, they want to examine how the economic base of any culture, and particularly of capitalist cultures, influences or determines the form and/or content of literature, both in general terms and in specific works of literature. They also want to look at how literature functions in relation to other aspects of the superstructure, particularly other articulations of ideology. Does literature reflect the economic base? If so, how? Does literature reflect other ideologies? If so, how? Do literary works create their own ideologies? If so, how are these ideologies related back to the economic base? And, finally, Marxist critics, like feminist critics, want to investigate how literature can work as a force for social change, or as a reaffirmation or 'reification' of existing conditions. Is literature part of the dialectical struggle that will end capitalism and bring about socialism, or is literature part of the bourgeois justification of capitalism?

According to Frederich Engels, ideology functions as an illusion; ideologies give people ideas about how to understand themselves and their lives, and these ideas disguise or mask what's really going on. In Engels's explanation, ideologies signify the way people live out their lives in class society, giving people the terms for the values, ideas, and images that tie them to their social functions, and thus prevent them from a true understanding of the real forces and relations of production. Ideology is thus an illusion which masks the real/objective situation; an example of this would be an ideology that tells you, as a worker, that the capitalists are really working in your interest, which disguises or hides the 'objective' reality that the capitalists' interests are opposed to the workers' interests. Engels says that the illusions created by ideology create *false consciousness* in people, who believe the ideological representations of how the world works and thus misperceive, or don't see at all, how the world objectively works in terms of the mode of production and the class divisions that mode of production creates. Workers, for Engels, are deluded by various kinds of ideology into thinking they're not exploited by the capitalist system, instead of seeing how they are.

In this view, literature is also a kind of illusion, a kind of ideology that prevents people from seeing the real relations of production at work. The earliest Marxist literary critics argued that a work of literature was entirely determined by the mode of production, by the economic base of the culture which produced it. This view, however, couldn't account for how or why literature might be able to challenge the ideological assumptions of a society; in this view, literature could only uphold the dominant cultural organization that produced it, rather than being a force for opposition or change.

Subsequent Marxist critics have argued that literature does something more complicated than simply 'reflecting' the values that support capitalism. According to Pierre Macheray, literature doesn't reflect either the economic base or other ideology, but rather it works on existing ideologies and transforms them, giving these ideologies new shape and structure; literature in Macheray's view is distinct from, and distant from, other forms of ideology and can provide insights into how ideologies are structured, and what their limits are. This view is also followed by Georg Lukacs, who argues that Marxist literary criticism should look at a work of literature in terms of the ideological structure(s) of which it is a part, but which it transforms in its art.

For other Marxists, including Bertolt Brecht, Walter Benjamin, and Louis Althusser, literature works the way any ideology does, by signifying the imaginary ways in which people perceive the real world; literature uses language to signify what it feels like to live in particular conditions, rather than using language to give a rational analysis of those conditions. Thus literature helps to *create* experience, not just reflect it. As a kind of ideology, literature for these critics is relatively autonomous, both of other ideological forms and of the economic base.

## LOUIS ALTHUSSER AND IDEOLOGY

Althusser is a structuralist Marxist. This should make you ask: How can that be? How can you combine Marxism, which relies on social/historical analysis, with structuralism, which relies on ahistorical/asocial analysis? Althusser answers that initially with distinction between ideologies (historical/social) and ideology (structural).

Althusser makes this distinction in his essay 'Ideology and Ideological State Apparatuses,' which discusses the relation between the state and its subjects. Althusser is asking why subjects are obedient, why people follow the laws, and why there isn't a revolt/ revolution against capitalism. His view of ideology and ideologies comes out of his understanding of the relations between state and subject, between government and citizens, so it's worthwhile to examine those ideas for a minute.

The state, for Althusser, is the kind of governmental formation that arises with capitalism. A state – you can substitute the word 'nation' here to help conceptualize the 'state' – is determined by the capitalist mode of production and formed to protect its interests. It is historically true, whether or not you are a Marxist, that the idea of nations as discrete units is coterminous with capitalism. It is also possible that democracy, as an ideology and/or a governmental form is also coterminous with capitalism, as democracy gives the 'illusion' that all people are equal, and have equal power, and hence masks relations of economic exploitation.

Althusser mentions two major mechanisms for insuring that people within a state behave according to the rules of that state, even when it's not in their best interests in regard to their class positions to do so. The first is what Althusser calls the RSAs, or Repressive State Apparatuses, that can enforce behavior directly, such as the police and the criminal justice system. Through these 'apparatuses' the state has the power to force you physically to behave. More importantly for literary studies, however, is the second mechanism Althusser investigates, which he calls ISAs, or Ideological State Apparatuses. These are institutions which generate ideologies which we as individuals (and groups) then internalize, and act in accordance with. These ISAs include schools, religions, the family, legal systems, politics, arts, sports – organizations that generate systems of ideas and values, which we as individuals believe (or don't believe). This is Althusser's main concern: How do we come to internalize, to believe, the ideologies that these ISAs create, and thus to misrecognize or misrepresent ourselves as unalienated subjects in capitalism.

Althusser's answer starts with the distinction between ideologies and ideology. *Ideologies* are specific, historical, and differing; we can talk about various ideologies, such as Christian ideology, democratic ideology, feminist ideology, and Marxist ideology. *Ideology*, however, is *structural*. Althusser says that ideology is a structure, and as such is 'eternal,' i.e. to be studied synchronically; this is why Althusser says that ideology has no history. He derives this idea of ideology as a structure from the Marxist idea that ideology is part of the superstructure, but he links the structure of ideology to the idea of the unconscious, from Freud and from Lacan. Because ideology is a structure, its contents will vary – you can fill it up with anything – but its form, like the structure of the unconscious, is always the same. And ideology works 'unconsciously.' Like language, ideology is a structure/system which we inhabit, which speaks us, but which gives us the illusion that we're in charge, that we freely chose the content of the things we believe, and that we can find lots of reasons why we believe those things.

Althusser's first premise is that 'Ideology is a "representation" of the Imaginary Relationship of Individuals to their Real conditions of existence.' He begins his explanation of this pronouncement by looking at why people need this imaginary relation to real conditions of existence. Why not just understand what is real?

Althusser's Marxist answer is that the material alienation of real conditions predisposes people to form representations which distance (alienate) them from these real conditions. In other words, the material relations of capitalist production are themselves alienating, but people can't quite deal with the harsh reality of this, so they make up stories about how the relations of production aren't so bad; these stories, or representations, then alienate them further from the real (alienating) conditions. The double distancing involved here, or the alienation of alienation, works like an analgesic, a pill, to keep us from feeling pain of alienation; if we didn't have these stories, we'd know the alienation of the real relations of production, and we'd probably revolt – or go mad.

These ideas about representation and reality assume that what is reflected in the imaginary representation of the world found in ideology is the 'real world,' or real conditions of existence. Althusser says that ideology doesn't represent the real world per se, but human beings' relation to that real world, to their perceptions of the real conditions of existence. In fact, we probably can't know the real world directly; what we know are always representations of that world, or representations of our relation to that world. Ideology, then, is the imaginary version, the represented version, the stories we tell ourselves about our relation to the real world.

So the 'real world' becomes not something that is objectively out there, but something that is the product of our relations to it, and of the ideological representations we make of it – the stories we tell ourselves about what is real become what is real. That's how ideology operates. In more Marxist terms, what ideology does is to present people with representations of their relations to relations of production, rather than with representations of the relations of production themselves.

Althusser's second thesis states that 'Ideology has a material existence.' It's important for Marxists always to be grounding their analysis in material practices, material relations; in order for Marxists to talk about ideas, we need to be able to talk about them as material, so that we don't lapse into idealism, or an argument that ideas are more 'real' than material objects. Althusser asserts that ideology is material by insisting that ideology always exists in two places – in an apparatus or practice (such as a ritual, or other forms of behavior dictated by the specific ideology) and in a subject, in a person – who is, by definition, material.

Althusser says that ideology, as material practice, depends on the notion of the subject. He states that 'there is no practice except by and in an ideology' and 'there is no ideology except by the subject and for subjects.' In short, there are no belief systems, and no practices determined by those belief systems, unless there is someone believing in and acting on those beliefs. This leads to Althusser's main question: How are individual subjects constituted in ideological structures? How does ideology create a notion of 'self' or subject?

All ideology has the function of constituting concrete individuals as subjects – of enlisting them in any belief system, according to Althusser. That's the main thing ideology as structure and ideologies as specific belief systems do: get people (subjects) to believe in them. There are three main points that Althusser makes about this process of becoming subjects-in-ideology.

1. We are born into subject-hood – if only because we're named before we're born; hence we're always already subjects. The acquisition of language is the process of becoming a subject, for both Althusser and Lacan.
2. We are always already subjects in ideology, in specific ideologies, which we inhabit, and which we recognize only as truth or obviousness. Everybody else's beliefs are recognizable as ideological, i.e. imaginary/illusory, whereas ours are simply true. Think, for example, about different religious beliefs. Everybody who believes in a religion thinks their religion is true, and everyone else's is just illusion, or ideology.
3. Ideology as structure gets us to become subjects, and not to recognize our subject positions within any particular ideological formation, through *interpellation*. Ideology interpellates individuals as subjects. The word 'interpellation' comes from the same root as the word 'appellation,' which means 'a name.' Interpellation is a hailing, according to Althusser. A particular ideology says, in effect, 'Hey you!' – and we respond, 'Me? You mean me?' And the ideology says, 'Yes, I mean you.'

You can see examples of this every day in commercials. I saw one the other night for a home gym system, claiming that 'this machine will give you the kind of workout you desire, meeting your needs better than any other home gym.' Each instance of 'you' in that ad was an interpellation – the ad seemed to address me personally, in order to get me to see myself as the 'you' being addressed, and hence to become a subject within its ideological structure.

Althusser makes some final points about ideology working this way to 'hail' us as subjects, so that we think these ideas are individually addressed to us, and hence are true. He says that ideology, as structure, requires not only subject but also Subject. In using the capital 'S,' he invokes an idea similar to that of Lacan, whom Althusser studied and wrote about, that there is a small-'s' subject, the individual person, and a capital 'S' Subject, which is the structural possibility of subjecthood which individuals fill. The idea of subject and Subject also suggests the duality of being a subject, where one is both the subject *of* language or ideology, as in being the subject of a sentence, and subject *to* ideology, having to obey its rules and laws and behave as that ideology dictates.

As you might be able to tell from the echoes of Lacan and Derrida, Althusser was a 'bricoleur' of other poststructuralist theorists. He was enchanted by Freud, and even more enchanted by Lacan; he links his ideas about ideology to Lacan directly, noting that the structure of ideology is specular, like Lacan's Imaginary, like the mirror stage.

Althusser's notion of the interpellation of the subject is directly useful to literary studies because it enables us to talk about how a literary text, as a subset or transformation or production of ideology (or of specific ideological formations) also constitutes us as subjects, and speaks to us directly. The most obvious form of how a literary text might interpellate us as subjects is one that uses direct address, when the text says 'dear reader,' as many pre-twentieth-century novels frequently do. All texts interpellate readers by some mechanism; all texts create subject positions for readers, whether that construction of subject positions is obvious or not.

## MIKHAIL BAKHTIN AND 'DISCOURSE IN THE NOVEL'

Bakhtin was not exactly a Marxist, but a theorist writing in the Soviet Union starting in the 1920s, and thus he was very much aware of Marxist theories and doctrines, and how they were being implemented. He was also associated with the school known as Russian Formalism, a kind of precursor to the American movement (in the 1940s and 1950s) called New Criticism. Bakhtin got in trouble with Soviet regime, was exiled, and did a lot of his best work in exile; because of his political conflicts with the Soviet Union, Bakhtin's works weren't translated into English until the 1970s. Bakhtin shares with Marxist theorists an interest in the historical and social world, an interest in how human beings act and think – in other words, an interest in the formation of the subject – and an interest in language as the means in which ideologies get articulated. For Bakhtin, as for Althusser, language itself, both structurally and in terms of content, is always ideological.

Language, for Bakhtin, is also always material. He would argue against Saussure and structuralist views of language which look only at the shape (or structure), and instead would argue that you always have to examine how people use language – how language as a material practice is always constituted by and through subjects. This is also Althusser's second thesis in 'Ideology and Ideological State Apparatuses.'

Bakhtin's theories focus primarily on the concept of dialogue, and on the notion that language – any form of speech or writing – is always *dialogic*. Dialogue consists of three elements: a speaker, a listener/respondent, and a relation between the two. Language, and what one says in language, are always thus the product of the interactions between (at least) two people. Bakhtin contrasts that notion of dialogue with the idea of the *monologic*, which are utterances by a single person or entity.

In his essay 'Discourse in the Novel' Bakhtin focuses on the question of literary forms or genres as examples of dialogic form. He focuses particularly on the contrast between poetry and novels. He says that poetry historically has always been the privileged form; you can think of this in terms of a binary opposition, poetry/fiction, where poetry is the valued term, and recall that most of the humanist literary theorists we looked at in Chapter 2 used poetry as their sole example of a literary form. We have also seen a version of this privileging in the poststructuralist theorists who, valuing the idea of play, plurality, or multiplicity in language, point to poetry as a place where language is more free, where the signifier and signified are the most disconnected. Bakhtin differs from Saussure, and from the tradition which emerges from Saussure, and which values the separation of signifier and signified more than the connection between the two. He was aware of Saussurean linguistics, and of structuralist theories in general, but Bakhtin, unlike almost all the other theorists we've read about so far, including Althusser, is not using Saussure's structuralist view of language.

Bakhtin begins his essay by posing a problem: If poetry is the more privileged literary form in Western culture, then what can you say about how language or discourse operates in novels? Clearly language operates differently, or is used differently, in fiction and in prose than in poetry; these genres have a different conception of how meaning is created than does poetry.

One answer to this question is that you can't, or shouldn't, talk about novels at all. For poststructuralist feminists such as Cixous, novels are part of a realist mode of representation, which is based on trying to connect linguistic signifiers to their referents, to 'real' signifieds; this, in Cixous's view, links fiction and realism to the attempt to make linear, fixed meaning, where one signifier is associated clearly with one and only one signified, which is what she calls masculine, or phallogocentric, writing.

From this perspective, any form of representational language – any prose discourse, and any forms of fiction – are part of the effort to make language stable, unitary, and determinant. And that's bad. From another perspective, however, there's no comparison between what novels do and what poetry does. Poetry is meant to be an art form, to be and to create something beautiful; fiction, on the other hand, is a kind of rhetoric, a literary form meant to persuade or to present an argument, not to produce an aesthetic effect. These definitions come largely from historical trends: the novel form comes from the prose traditions of rhetorical persuasion. Poetry is not without its didactic function, certainly; as many critics from Sir Philip Sidney on have noted, the purpose of art is 'to delight and to instruct.' But generally poetry has been associated with the aesthetic function ('delight') and novels with the didactic function ('instruct').

Bakhtin starts with this division between poetry and prose fiction, and their social functions, in order to reconceptualize the idea of the way stylistics has privileged poetry. He says that rhetoric – the art of using language to persuade or convince people – has always been subordinated in Western culture to poetry, because rhetoric has a social purpose: it does something. Poetry, despite Sidney's claim to the contrary, has always functioned almost exclusively on an aesthetic level. Poetry is like a painting that hangs on the wall; prose is like a piece of kitchen machinery, in Bakhtin's view.

Because it does something, Bakhtin says, fiction, as a subset of rhetoric, has positive qualities. First of all, it is a socially and historically specific form of language use. A novel, Bakhtin argues, has more in common at any particular historical moment with other existing forms of rhetoric – with the languages used in journalism, in ethics, in religion, in politics, in economics, for example – than poetry does. In fact, Bakhtin says, the novel is more oriented toward the social/historical forms of rhetoric than toward the particular artistic or aesthetic ideas present at any particular moment, while poetry focuses primarily on aesthetic concerns and only secondarily (if at all) on other aspects of social existence.

Bakhtin says that ideas about language have always postulated a unitary speaker, a speaker who has an unmediated relation to 'his unitary and singular "own" language.' This speaker (kind of like

Derrida's 'engineer') says, 'I produce unique meaning in my own speech; my speech comes from me alone.' Bakhtin says this way of thinking about language posits language as a system in contrast to the individual who speaks it. Both system and speaker, however, produce what Bakhtin calls monologic language–language that seems to come from a single, unified source.

Bakhtin opposes monologic language to *heteroglossia*, which is the idea of a multiplicity of languages all in operation in a culture. Heteroglossia might be defined as the collection of all the forms of social speech, or rhetorical modes, that people use in the course of their daily lives. A good example of heteroglossia would be all the different languages you use in the course of a day. You talk to your friends in one way, to your professor or employer another way, to your parents or children in a third way, to a waiter in a restaurant in a fourth way, and so on.

Bakhtin says that there are actually two forces in operation whenever language is used: centripetal force and centrifugal force. Centripetal force tends to push things toward a central point; centrifugal force tends to push things away from a central point and out in all directions. Bakhtin says that monologic language (monologia) operates according to centripetal force: the speaker of monologic language is trying to push all the elements of language, all of its various rhetorical modes (the journalistic, the religious, the political, the economic, the academic, the personal) into one single form or utterance, coming from one central point. The centripetal force of monologia is trying to get rid of differences among languages (or rhetorical modes) in order to present one unified language. Monologia is a system of norms, of one standard language, or an 'official' language, a standard language that everyone would have to speak, and which would then be enforced by various mechanisms, such as Althusser's RSAs and ISAs.

Heteroglossia, on the other hand, tends to move language toward multiplicity – not, as with the other poststructuralist theorists, in terms of multiplicity of meaning for individual words or phrases, by disconnecting the signifier and the signified, but by including a wide variety of different ways of speaking, different rhetorical strategies and vocabularies.

Both heteroglossia and monologia, both the centrifugal and centripetal forces of language, Bakhtin says, are always at work in any utterance: 'Every concrete utterance of a speaking subject serves as a point where centrifugal as well as centripetal forces are brought to bear.'[1] Language, in this sense, is always both anonymous and social, something formed beyond any individual, but also concrete, filled with specific content which is shaped by the speaking subject.

Poetic language, Bakhtin argues, has been conceptualized historically as centripetal, and novelistic language as centrifugal. Novelistic language is dialogic and heteroglossic, Bakhtin says, and as such it exists as a site of struggle to overcome, or at least to parody, the univocal, monologic utterances that characterize official centralized language.

Bakhtin wants to find alternatives to a strict formalist or structuralist approach, because these ways of looking at literature tend to examine a literary work 'as if it were a hermetic and self-sufficient whole, whose elements constitute a closed system presuming nothing beyond themselves, no other utterances.'[2] Bakhtin argues that poetry is fundamentally monologic, and operates as if it were a 'hermetic and self-sufficient whole,' which is why formalist critics, like the American New Critics, mostly studied poetry, not fiction. The poetic word, according to Bakhtin, acknowledges only itself, its object (what it represents), and its own unitary and singular language; the word in poetry encounters only the problem of its relation to an object, not its relation to another's word. Put simply, words used poetically refer to language itself, but not to non-poetic language, to other languages in the culture.

The poetic word – Bakhtin calls it 'autotelic,' which means 'coming from itself,' 'referring to itself' – has meaning only in itself, or in relation to an object as signifier or in relation to a signified. As Bakhtin puts it, all the activity of the poetic word is exhausted by the relation between word and object; poetry is therefore the use of words without reference to history. 'It presumes nothing beyond the borders of its own context (except, of course, what can be found in the treasure-house of language itself).'[3] The poetic word means only itself as word, or it can include all its connotative and denotative meanings (the 'treasure-house of language'); when it refers to an object, that object is cut off from any social or historical specificity. In other words, a poetic word is only a signifier, or, when it's connected to a signified, that signified is always an abstraction. So in a poem the word 'bottle' will refer only to itself, or to the idea of 'bottle,' rather than to a specific bottle, like the water bottle I may be drinking from right now.

Let me give you a specific example. Let's say you find a piece of paper with these words written on it: 'Two pounds ground beef, seedless grapes, loaf bread.' You would most likely assume that someone had dropped a grocery list. But what if you found the signature 'T. S. Eliot' at the bottom of the page? Could this be a poem?

You could certainly do a close reading of it, searching for its meaning as if it were a poem. Such a reading might focus on the first word, 'Two,' as implying a fundamental duality, but that duality is undermined by the form of the verb 'pounds,' which, as a verb, is singular. The idea of 'pounds' as verb brings up an image of violence, that the 'Two' in the first word might be in some kind of struggle. That struggle might be against the 'ground,' the third word, which connotes an image of violence – something being 'ground.' It also rhymes with 'pound' – so the 'two' who are also 'one' (singular in the verb) are pounding the ground in some kind of anger. What's the ground? The ground of their being, the ground they stand on, the ground that divides them as one/two beings? Then 'beef' – well, 'beef' can mean 'meat,' the basic substance of human flesh, or it can mean 'argument,' which fits with the image of the two pounding the ground (or each other) in this fury. The next line gives us the reason for their anger. Not only are they divided, not quite one and not quite two, but they are 'seedless' – no offspring, no fertility, no reproduction. This is perhaps the source of the violence in the first line. The idea of the fight is echoed then in the word 'grapes,' which brings up 'sour grapes,' feeling resentful for something you can't have, as well as echoing the word 'gripe,' which, like 'beef,' gives the idea of a quarrel. 'Seedless grapes' is also an oxymoron, a paradox, like 'two pounds;' grapes are fruit, hence a symbol of natural abundance, yet they are seedless, sterile. The last line, 'loaf bread,' reinforces the idea of a fruitless reproduction causing violence; the word 'bread' echoes the word 'bred,' associated with reproduction again, and 'loaf' implies laziness or inability, which stands in contrast to the action of 'pound'ing in the first line. So the lazy loafers are the ones who have bread/bred, who have engaged successfully in reproduction, while the fighters, who struggle, are the sterile ones – and their sterility is a product of their lack of differentiation, their inability to decide whether they are one or two, the same or different.

This is completely silly, of course. But it's possible. This, Bakhtin would say, is how poetry is monologic: if we assume these words are a poem, we read them quite differently than if we assume these words are a grocery list. The writer or critic interested in seeing the heteroglossia in language would read these words as embedded in social relations; such a critic would probably read them as a grocery list, as writing with a distinct social purpose, rather than as abstractions.

But Bakhtin would also say that the 'poetic' reading of the grocery list also has validity; the words on the page never mean only the object they signify. In poetry, the social meaning is almost entirely erased, but in fiction the social meaning and the abstract meaning (the 'autotelic' meaning) are both present. Novelists might show someone writing this grocery list, and on one level that list would simply be an itemization of foods the character will buy, but there might also be a symbolic level, where these particular foods have significance or resonance beyond the merely literal. As Bakhtin says, the prose artist 'elevates the social heteroglossia surrounding objects into an image that has finished contours, an image completely shot through with dialogized overtones.'[4]

Bakhtin discusses further the idea of the dialogic, arguing that all words or utterances are directed toward an answer, a response. In everyday speech, words are understood by being taken into the listener's own conceptual system, filled with specific objects and emotional expressions, and being related to these; the understanding of an utterance is thus inseparable from the listener's response to it. All speech is thus oriented toward what Bakhtin calls the 'conceptual horizon' of the listener; this horizon comprises the various social languages the listener inhabits/uses. Dialogism is an orientation toward the interaction between the various languages of a speaker and the languages of a listener. Bakhtin says that 'discourse lives on the boundary between its own context and another, alien, context.'[5]

Bakhtin argues that the sense of boundedness, historicity, and social determination found in dialogic notions of language is alien to poetic style. The writer of prose is always attuned to her own language(s) and alien languages (i.e. the languages of listeners), and uses heteroglossia – employs a variety of languages – to always be entering into dialogue with readers. The fiction writer is always directing her 'speech' (i.e. writing) toward the possible responses of readers, and is always trying to find more things to say, more ways to say it, so that readers can understand the message(s).

This diversity of voices which is heteroglossia is the fundamental characteristic of prose writers, and of the novel as a genre. A good example of a heteroglossic novel is Melville's *Moby-Dick*, which uses a huge variety of (socio-ideological) languages: the language of the whaling industry, the language of Calvinist religion, the language of the domestic/sentimental novel, the language of Shakespearean drama, the language of Platonic philosophy, the language of democracy, etc. In using all these languages, Melville hopes to increase the potential size of his readership, as the novel probably contains some kind of language which every reader has as part of her existing vocabulary or 'horizon.'

## MICHEL FOUCAULT: DISCOURSE, POWER/KNOWLEDGE, AND THE AUTHOR FUNCTION

Both Althusser and Bakhtin are interested, in the largest sense, in examining how ideology, and literature as a specialized subset of ideology, gets you to do things; both are interested in questions of why subjects obey the law, why workers don't rebel against exploitation, and why we don't resist any and all kinds of unifying or centralized authority.

Michel Foucault is also interested in exploring the mechanisms that create and enforce your obedience to authoritative rule. Unlike Althusser or Bakhtin, Foucault is not a Marxist, structuralist, deconstructionist, psychoanalyst, feminist, or any other 'ist,' though he's familiar with developments in all of these; as a poststructrualist theorist, he is in a category all his own. Foucault is *Foucault* the way Freud is *Freud*: the founder of a school of thought, a way of thinking about how the world (and literary texts which are part of the world) operate.

Foucault is primarily interested in examining how *discourse* creates relationships of *power/knowledge* which then become the framework within which human thought and action are possible. For Foucault, ideology is always expressed in discourse, in texts produced as knowledge about a certain topic or area. These discourses create the possible ways we can think about a topic, and also create the methods/practices we have for dealing with that topic.

A discourse is the conglomeration of all the kinds of writing, talking, thinking, and acting on or about a certain topic. Let's take blindness as our example. Doctors write about it, psychologists, teachers, legal experts (think about the concept of being 'legally blind'), poets, novelists, all these people produce writings (texts) that give some definition of blindness, some portrait of it. Some may address what causes it, some may address what cures it, some may address what problems blindness creates for individuals or for institutions, some may give personal histories of blind people or fictional accounts of the symbolic meaning of blindness. The 'discourse' on blindness would consist of all the texts written about the ideas of blindness in our culture, from every possible discipline or perspective. Together, these writings form what we know about blindness, and that knowledge informs what we do and think and say about blindness.

For Foucault, all social practice stems from discourse. Writings about blindness from the eighteenth century to the present have insisted that blind people, because they lack sight, have an increased sense of hearing, and that because of that they must be more musically inclined than sighted people. From those writings came the idea, the knowledge, that blindness = musicality, and thus the practice that education for blind people should focus on developing their musical ability, providing job opportunities in music careers (like piano tuning), and allowing blind people to be composers and musicians. The discursive construction of blindness informed what social relationships and possibilities blind people could have.

Foucault is interested in how discourse shapes the relations between power and knowledge; he sees power/knowledge as inseparable – but not, it is important to note, as binary opposites. He argues that all operations of 'power' – all the means by which one entity gets another entity to do, to be, and/or to act a certain way – are based on these discursive forms of knowledge. The best example of this is the frequently-heard phrase 'Studies have shown that . . .' Studies – that is, knowledge produced by people who have been acknowledged as experts – show that, i.e. produce some discursive form of knowledge that then becomes the basis for action: as with the legislature, with policy decisions, with institutional practices, etc.

That's the 'knowledge' side of power/knowledge. Now we need to discuss Foucault's idea of power. Power is usually conceived of as a form of repression, like Althusser's RSAs – some force that keeps you in line via threat of punishment. But for Foucault, power operates much more like Althusser's ISAs – like ideology itself. Power is productive, not repressive; it creates situations, relationships, and subjects, rather than just punishing them. And the goal of power, like Althusser's ideology, is to create subjects who act properly on their own, who don't need the police or other enforcement agencies to use physical forms of restraint or punishment to get them to behave. Foucault, like Althusser, is interested in the creation of 'good' subjects who obey the rules (whatever they are) because they've internalized a belief in the truth of those rules, and 'bad' subjects who disobey because they don't believe them. And Foucault says that discourse, like ideology, and like a literary text, indeed like any text, produces subject positions which then govern any individual's choices, understanding of reality, actions, and beliefs.

Foucault is particularly interested in how discourse creates relations of power/knowledge concerning human bodies. Such discourse then works to regulate how bodies function, how we think of them, and how we understand our own bodies. He particularly focuses on questions of health and illness, sanity and madness, law-abiding and criminal actions/bodies, and normal and deviant sexualities. To go back to the example of the discourse on blindness, the producers of knowledge about blindness, such as the directors of schools and institutions for the blind and doctors who specialized in blindness, argued in the nineteenth century that lack of sight produced lack of physical motion, and lack of motion produced physically weak bodies (bodies described specifically as pale, thin, twisted, and immobile) which meant bodies that were not fit for any kind of physical labor. The bodies of the blind – not just their eyesight, but their whole bodies – were thus defined as weak and inferior and unproductive, and schools and institutions put together curricula and programs designed to 'correct' the weaknesses of the blind perscu's body and to train blind people in trades which would minimize their physical deficiencies. Hence, again, these schools emphasized musical education as not requiring a strong body, and as work that blind bodies could thus perform for pay.

So the big question for Foucault is: How do discourses create subjects, and particularly bodies, that behave well, that are 'good' and follow the rules?

One of the reasons you are 'good,' according to what Foucault talks about in *Discipline and Punish*, is that you think you might be caught not being good, and thus be punished. Foucault talks about a society based on surveillance – a kind of power/knowledge – which he says is typified by the 'Panopticon.' He talks about the way that prisons were designed in the eighteenth century: rather than having individual cells where each prisoner was locked away from everyone else, like in a dungeon, the new model of prison featured cells that were highly visible, and a central tower from which guards or authorities watched the prisoners. The central tower is the Panopticon, the position from which every prisoner in every cell can constantly be watched. The prisoner in a cell, meanwhile, can only see the Panopticon, not any of the other cells; further, the prisoner can't see into the Panopticon to see whether anyone is watching him or not. The prisoner's behavior is thus regulated not by guards with guns, but by the prisoner's own awareness that he is always being watched.

Our Western contemporary culture is regulated by panoptical mechanisms; there are surveillance devices everywhere, including false cameras that make you think they are real so that you don't do anything bad. One of these mechanisms is photoradar: if you speed or fail to stop for a red light, you might not get pulled over by a cop, but rather receive a ticket in the mail a week later. That's the current epitome of the Panopticon, of Foucault's society wherein subjects behave because they never know when 'Big Brother' may be watching. The punishment – the traffic ticket – becomes automatic and impersonal. If a cop had stopped you, you might have been able to talk him or her out of giving you a ticket; with photoradar, with the automated Panopticon, the mechanisms for recording and punishing violations of rules are designed to work without any human characteristics, without the necessity of a human operator at all.

Foucault points out that the constant circulation of power/ knowledge is never one-sided or unidirectional, however. Power comes from exchange – the exchange of goods, the exchange of people, and the exchange of ideas. Wherever there is power working in one direction, there is always a counterforce of power working in resistance to it; whenever one network of exchange creates a disciplinary mechanism (such as photoradar), those subjected to it create, via their own networks of exchange, modes of resistance or ways to foil the panoptical vigilance. Thus discourse and practice, at the institutional and individual levels, are always in dialectical interplay, according to Foucault.

## NOTES

1   Mikhail Bakhtin, 'Discourse in the Novel,' in Hazard Adams and Leroy Searle, eds, *Critical Theory Since 1965*. Gainesville, FL: University Press of Florida, 1986, p. 668.
2   *Ibid.*, p. 668.
3   *Ibid.*, p. 671.
4   *Ibid.*, p. 671.
5   *Ibid.*, p. 673.

## SUGGESTIONS FOR FURTHER READING

Lydia Alix Fillingham, *Foucault for Beginners*. New York: Writers and Readers Publishing Inc., 1994.
Gary Gutting, *Foucault: A Very Short Introduction*. Oxford: Oxford University Press, 2005.
Michael Holquist, *Dialogism*. New York: Routledge, 2002.
Rius, *Marx for Beginners*. New York: Pantheon, 1990.
Peter Singer, *Marx: A Very Short Introduction*. Oxford: Oxford University Press, 2001.
Sue Vice, *Introducing Bakhtin*. Manchester: Manchester University Press, 1998.
Rupert Woodfin, *Introducing Marxism*. New York: Totem Books, 2004.

# CHAPTER 9

# RACE AND POSTCOLONIALISM

When someone asks me what I do for a living, I reply that I'm an English professor. Many people then make some comment about watching their grammar, as if 'English' denoted the field of studying correct grammar, spelling, and composition, and as if my job were to correct the grammar of everyone I spoke with. Rarely does anyone, on hearing my distinctly American accent, assume that I am saying that I am a professor of English nationality. Most people know that an 'English professor' and an 'English department' in a university study works of literature in English. The designation 'English' for this field of knowledge, however, raises a host of questions about the relationships among nationality, language, and literary production.

The field we call 'English' was originally defined based on the equation between nationality and language: an 'English' department studies works of literature written in the English language by people whose cultural history could be traced directly back to England. What is 'English' is what has been claimed by England as belonging to English culture, as well as the island of Britain itself: hence Scotland, Wales, Ireland, the United States, Canada, Australia, India, and parts of Africa and East Asia have been, at one time or another in Western history, considered 'English' or British. The field of postcolonial theory examines the effect that colonialism has had on the development of literature and literary studies – on novels, poems, and 'English' departments – within the context of the history and politics of regions under the influence, but outside the geographical boundaries, of England and Britain.

## COLONIALISM AND 'ENGLISH'

From the late seventeenth century to the middle of the twentieth century, Britain extended its national rule to countries and areas all over the world: to North America, to Africa, to the Middle East, to India, to Asia, to the West Indies, South America, and Polynesia, creating British colonies in these lands and, in most cases, taking over the administration of government, so that British laws and customs ruled the people who lived half a world away from the Britain itself. As a US citizen, I was raised on the story of how 'America' rebelled against being governed by a distant land, and fought a war to become independent of British rule. US history as a British colony is somewhat unique, however, as 'we' – meaning the people who became 'Americans' when the nation of the United States was founded – were formerly British citizens who succeeded so well in colonizing the coastal regions of North America, and in subduing the indigenous population of Native Americans, that we shifted national identification away from Britain and named ourselves something else (Americans).

Most of the British colonies of the eighteenth and nineteenth centuries did not rebel and form their own nations – largely because the people of those nations were non-whites, non-Western people. British colonial rule, and that of all other Western nations who formed colonies, such as France and Germany, depended on seeing the indigenous populations of these colonized areas as inferior, as therefore needing the 'advanced civilization' offered by Western culture. In fact, as Edward Said argues, the West (or Occident) *produced* the non-white, non-Western cultures and peoples as inferior through a variety of discourses which stated the terms of their existence as inferior.

One of the impetuses for colonization was, of course, the spread of capitalism: colonies offered sources of raw materials, cheap labor, and new markets for Western goods, and the history of colonialism is very much caught up in the economics of capitalism. But colonialism couldn't be confined merely to the economic realm: when a nation like Britain colonized a non-Western region, it exported its own legal, religious, educational, military, political, and aesthetic ideas along with its economic regime – what Marx would call the superstructure, and Althusser would call the Ideological State Apparatus, or ISA. In places like Africa and India, British colonial rule meant teaching the indigenous people about the superiority of

Western practices: through setting up systems of police and courts and legislatures following British laws, through sending missionaries to convert natives to Christianity (largely the Church of England) and establishing churches and seminaries, and through setting up schools to teach British customs, British history, and the English language to children and adults, in order to make them more like British citizens. And with these ideological exportations came British/Western 'culture,' in the form of music, art, and literature – so that, regardless of the ancient literary traditions of India, China, or the Arab world, inhabitants of these colonized areas were taught that Chaucer, Shakespeare, and Milton were the 'greatest' authors who ever wrote. In short, British cultural standards were upheld and all other notions of culture, of art or literature or philosophy, were denounced as inferior and subordinated to Western standards.

This is part of what an 'English' department was originally designed to do – to study and to assert the mastery of 'English' literature as the most important literature (of the most important and advanced civilization) ever known. 'English' departments were thus part of establishing the hegemony (meaning the dominance) of British culture worldwide. English departments also served as a regulatory mechanism to teach and enforce the 'correct' form of English as a language, making sure that educated people all spoke and wrote in the same grammatically acceptable forms. An 'English' department, and its professors, thus historically have functioned to uphold the dominance of a *monologic* form of the English language, just as they have upheld English literature as the universal standard of literary excellence.

## HENRY LOUIS GATES, JR AND 'THE SIGNIFYING MONKEY'

There's a strong connection between postcolonial theories and contemporary African-American theories, as both look at how a hegemonic white/Western culture came to dominate a non-white culture, and at how the subordinated culture reacted to and resisted that domination. The history of black–white relations in the United States is quite different from that in Britain, because in the US whites imported blacks from Africa as slaves, rather than urging whites to go and settle in Africa to 'civilize' the indigenous peoples. But while the dynamics of racial and cultural politics are different, some of the effects are the same: in the United States, slavery and racism produced a hegemonic white culture which enforced its systems and values on the non-white population, and that non-white population both obeyed and resisted those systems and values. Both postcolonial theories and African-American theories about US racial dynamics argue that the colonized 'other' learns to speak what W. E. B. DuBois has called a 'double-voiced' discourse, speaking both the language (in Bakhtin's terms) of the dominant culture and the language of the subordinated culture.

Henry Louis Gates's article 'The Blackness of Blackness: A Critique of the Sign and the Signifying Monkey' examines a particular mode of speech, a Bakhtinian 'language' or sociolect, arising within African-American communities. Gates begins the article by discussing the term 'signifying,' which is familiar to literary theorists since Saussure; we know 'signification' as the relationship between signifier and signified which creates a sign. Gates points out, however, that the term has an entirely different meaning, and history, in African-American cultural usage. He is using an idea explored by Bakhtin and his colleague V. N. Volosinov about ideas about the multi-accentuality of a sign, the idea that a single word or sign might have radically different meanings in different contexts. Within the context of academic theory-speak, 'signifying' means what Saussure laid out; within an African-American cultural context, however, 'signifying,' or 'signifyin,'" is a name for a particular linguistic practice, which Gates links to 'the dozens,' calling out, rapping, and testifying.

Gates's analysis of signifyin' bridges the gap between the academic dominant-cultural context of the term and the African-American subordinated context; he uses academic discourse, in talking about Saussure, and about classical rhetoric, to support the idea that the African-American (or 'black') practice of signifyin' is just as historically significant, and just as complex, as any dominant cultural linguistic practice. In other words, Gates insists that signifyin' or rapping is not just how African-Americans talk because they're not well educated or don't know about 'correct' (i.e. hegemonic dominant cultural, or 'white') forms of speech; rather, the activity of signifyin' comes from an African and African-American tradition, just as classical rhetoric comes from the tradition of Greek and Latin modes of speech. He thus traces the roots of black signifying to African mythology and religious beliefs; more specifically, he looks at a figure called the 'Signifying Monkey' as the archetype and origin of the practice of signifying in the African-American community.

'Signifying,' according to the *Oxford Companion to African American Literature*, is a form of verbal play, centering primarily on the insult, whereby people can demonstrate a mastery of improvisational rhyme and rhythm; the demonstration of such verbal mastery is a mechanism for empowerment within communities where other forms of power – political, economic – are unavailable. Gates links this practice to the mythological figure of the Signifying Monkey, who is able to trick the more powerful animals in the jungle through his verbal skills. Gates points out that the link between the Signifying Monkey and the practice of signifying works in at least two directions: the figure, and the practice, come directly from African cultural mythology, and variants can be found in virtually all communities with African origins; and the figure of the Monkey in particular plays on the racist construction of Africans as like apes, therefore less human than whites. The Signifying Monkey thus takes a trope, a figure, from the white racist idea of blackness and reaccentuates it, renames it, signifies on it, so that 'monkey' no longer means an inferior, i.e. black, person, but rather represents a person with verbal power and the ability to stir up conflict between those who have more social power than he does.

Gates places the Signifying Monkey at the borders of 'correct,' i.e. hegemonic, dominant cultural forms of speech. You might think of the Signifying Monkey in this way as a subject position within language. That position, like the 'feminine' position we discussed in Cixous's feminist theory, is further away from a center where language is fixed, stable, and univocal; at the margins of language or discourse, speech is more fluid, more flexible, more able to 'play' in Derrida's sense. The Signifying Monkey, then, as a linguistic subject, is more able to use words with greater flexibility, to 'trope' and play and signify and shift meanings, than the speaker who stands closer to the center of language.

This should start to sound pretty familiar. We've been talking all along about the two poles of language: the pole where meaning is fixed and stable, where a word means one thing and one thing only; and the pole where meaning is fluid, and words can have multiple, ambiguous, and indefinite meanings. All the theorists we've read have talked about the advantages and disadvantages of fixed vs fluid meaning. Theories of race and postcolonialism, like most of the poststructuralist theories we've read, uphold the idea that fixity of meaning is associated with rigid systems of thought and government, and fluidity of meaning, play, is associated with systems of thought and government that favor multiplicity and multiculturalism. And, like most of the theories we've been reading, postcolonial theories say that fluidity and play and multiplicity is better, in all kinds of ways, than fixity and rigidity. In explaining the figure of the Signifying Monkey as a subject who plays with language in order to undermine rigid systems of racial dominantion, Gates celebrates the subversive power of fluid language to disrupt existing hierarchies which create binary relations of domination and subordination.

## POSTCOLONIALISM AND ORIENTALISM

Postcolonial theory takes on the politics of the study of 'English' literature and culture from the perspective of those who were colonized by it. Postcolonial theory would ask whether an 'English department' necessarily reinforces the hegemony of Western cultural practices and thus supports the political and economic forces which have subordinated what we have come to call the 'third world.'

Postcolonial theorists and scholars argue a lot about the meaning of the word 'postcolonial,' and particularly about when a 'postcolonial' theory or literature begins to emerge. Does the 'post' of postcolonial begin with national independence? With economic independence from the colonizing country? With cultural independence? In US history, we are taught that 'America' became an independent nation on July 4, 1776, when the Declaration of Independence was signed. But the Revolutionary War still had to be fought to assert that claim of national independence, and to be followed, for emphasis, with the War of 1812, before the US was internationally recognized as a nation independent from Britain. Even then, US economics were closely linked to British manufacturing, and US artists and authors spent a great deal of effort throughout the nineteenth century in trying to establish a clear distinction between British and American literature, and to proclaim the quality of the latter with minimal reference to the former.

So when does a colony become postcolonial? For this book, we'll take the easy definition: postcolonial designates the time after official colonial rule. For most former British colonies, postcoloniality begins in the mid- to late twentieth century, when most of the British colonies, such as India, fought for their independence from the British Empire, and became separate nations. Postcolonial theories begin to arise in the 1960s as thinkers from the former colonies began to create their own forms of knowledge, their own discourses, to counter the discourses of colonialism: these postcolonial discourses articulated the experience of the colonized, rather than the colonizer, giving what's called the 'subaltern' – the subordinated non-white, non-Western subject of colonial rule – a voice. Postcolonial theorists examine how Western cultures, the colonizers, created the colonial subject, the subaltern, through various discursive practices, and examine also how subaltern cultures both participated in and worked to resist colonization, through various overt or covert, direct or subversive, means.

Postcolonial theory is thus centrally concerned with examining the mechanisms through which the colonizing powers persuaded the colonized people to accept a foreign culture as 'better' than their own indigenous methods of government and social organization. Among the most important kinds of power/knowledge brought by the colonizers was the construction of the concept of 'race,' and more specifically the racial binary opposition of 'white' and 'other' – be that other 'black,' 'yellow,' 'brown,' 'red,' or whatever other color became the signifier for the 'otherness' of the colonized people. In the case of the United States, the 'native' population (once the Native Americans had been colonized or killed) was itself defined as white, a fact which deprived the colonizing British of a dominant form of power/knowledge which worked successfully with non-white colonies to produce their native inhabitants as inferior.

Race and postcolonial theorists are interested in studying how distinctions based on race are made, circulated, and enforced. When you think about how you know what race someone belongs to, usually you will think about the physical or biological traits that supposedly mark 'race,' such as hair color, eye color and skin color. These traits or markers show that the concept of 'race' is actually a signifying system, wherein certain physiological facts become signifiers connected to specific ideological signifieds. Within the system of 'race,' a dark skin color becomes a signifier, and the signified it is connected to might be 'athletic ability' or 'musical talent.' The connections of physical signifiers to ideological signifieds in this system is 'racism' – and you can come up with your own examples of how pejorative the signifieds can be that *get* connected to a particular physiological signified.

'Race,' as a genetic or biological construct, does not exist. Rather, it is a signifying system wherein physical signifiers become connected with concepts of ability to create the 'meaning' of one's 'race' appearance. As in any signifying system, these connections are *arbitrary*; there is no essential or provable connection between the physical signifiers of 'race' and the cultural conceptions (and misconceptions) which we assume those physical signifiers point to.

The question for theorists of race, then, is how these arbitrary connections between signifiers and signifieds *get* made, enforced, expanded, reproduced, and/or modified. The answer that most give is Foucault's idea of discourse. Writings about race, coming from the disciplines of anthropology, sociology, psychology, criminology, biology, medicine, and (of course) literary studies connect a certain kind of eye shape with a certain kind of intelligence, or a hair texture with a social behavior. That is how 'racial traits' are created, elaborated, and perpetuated. And when we have made those associations, connected certain signifiers with certain signifieds, we then view those signs of race as 'real,' as 'true,' as 'factual.'

Edward Said's *Orientalism* is one of the foundational studies of how signifiers *get* connected to signifieds through discursive means to create the ordering system we call 'race.' Following Foucault, Said argues that discourse works to create 'knowledge' about a supposed 'racial' group. The best example of this is what anthropology used to be: a discipline to create knowledge, from the perspective of the dominant (usually Western) culture, about the subordinated/colonized culture. This knowledge wielded power, as it defined and described a culture or racial group, and thus produced the social attitudes, the ideologies and practices, which surrounded and delimited the group or culture being written about.

Said uses the word 'orientalism' to refer to the set of discursive practices, the forms of power/knowledge, that Western Anglo-European cultures used to produce (and hence control) a region of the globe known as 'the Orient.' You might want to take a moment to think about the stereotypes associated with the word 'Orient' and 'Oriental,' all of which labeled 'the Orient' as a place of mystery and exoticism. Such 'otherness' exists in relation to the familiarity of the Western Anglo-European world; the basis of 'orientalism,' like the basis of any form of racism or ethnocentrism, is the idea that 'we' are 'selves' who are 'familiar,' and that 'others' are necessarily 'exotic.'

'Orientalism' depends upon the binary opposition 'occident/ orient,' meaning 'west/east' – but from whose perspective? How are 'east' and 'west' determined in the discursive construction of 'occident' and 'orient?' The answer, of course, is that 'the orient' is whatever is east of the Anglo-European perspective. 'Orient' and 'Occident' are a product of the ways that Anglo-European explorers drew the map of the world from the seventeenth century onward. Said points out that maps are not just representations of a 'real world' that is out there, a way to locate where rivers and mountains are. Rather, maps are texts which, like literary texts, carry with them a cultural perspective and work to create an ideologically-based reality.

An example of this is how the world figures time. In international time, there's a 24-hour clock, and the earth is divided into 24 'time zones.' Where does time begin? In Greenwich, England, 0:00 is midnight GMT, or Greenwich Mean Time, and the rest of the world measures time in relation to GMT. The same idea works with longitude: zero degrees longitude, the 'starting point' of global navigation, runs just east of London.

In both of these examples, England is the center of the world, the place where time and space begin, the starting point for all other models of mapping. And that's because England drew the maps and created the time-measuring system. And that's because England was the largest colonial power in the modern world (from the eighteenth century to the middle of the nineteenth century), and had the power to create the knowledge of the entire globe.

Said's work outlines how the cultural knowledge about, and representations of, 'the Orient' and 'the oriental' constructed by the West produce 'the Orient' as a place of 'otherness.' When we list the (racist) associations our Anglo-European culture makes with the concept of 'oriental,' what we're doing is listing all the things that our culture doesn't want to have defining us. For example, we might hear 'oriental' and think 'opium-smoking, heathen, mysterious, exotic' – all terms which are negative when compared to their binary opposites: sober, Christian, known, familiar. Said argues that the West's construction of the Orient projects all the things that the West considers negative, all the things that have to be repressed – all the things on the right-hand side of the slash in a binary opposition – onto our construct of the other, the Orient. So 'the Orient' becomes the place where body (as opposed to mind), evil (as opposed to good), and the feminine (as opposed to masculine) all reside. By placing all of these forms of 'otherness' on the Orient, Said says, the Occident can construct itself as all positive.

Examples of the West's projection of otherness onto the idea of the Orient or the oriental appear all over the place in Western popular culture, from the Charlie Chan movies all the way to *The Karate Kid* series. The character of Mr Miyagi represents the American assumptions about a typical Japanese man: he is asexual, has no wife or girlfriend, cultivates bonsai trees, practices martial arts, speaks in broken sentences inflected with a heavy accent (despite having lived in California for 30 years!) and has 'inscrutable' behaviors, such as catching flies with chopsticks.

The history of imperialism is the history of discourses about colonized places, whether in the form of official government reports, personal travel narratives, or imaginative fiction set in 'exotic' foreign lands. You might think about Joseph Conrad's *Heart of Darkness* as an example of imperial discourse – and as a novel which shows the contradictions and the collapse of imperial forms of power/knowledge. Said argues that the creation of discourse about a colonized culture, about 'the other,' works also to silence that colonized culture, which cannot 'talk back,' or write about itself. Rather, such discourse renders the people of the colonized culture the powerless subjects of Western power/knowledge, and anything the colonized culture tries to say or write about itself is by definition considered illegitimate, non-knowledge, nonsense.

Postcolonial literary studies, and postcolonial theory in general, focus on what happens when the formerly colonized culture starts to, or insists on, producing its own knowledge about itself. What happens when 'the empire writes back' to the dominant culture, when the silenced subjects of knowledge insist on becoming the producers of knowledge? One way to think about this is via deconstruction. The discourses that create the colonizers as the knowers and the colonized as the subjects of knowledge all depend on our old friend, the structure of binary oppositions, including West/East, Occident/Orient, civilized/native, self/other, educated/ignorant, etc. When 'the empire writes back,' these binary oppositions are deconstructed; when a colonized subject insists on taking up the position of 'self,' as the creator of knowledge about his or her own culture, rather than as the subject of that knowledge, these binary oppositions start to fall apart.

## HOMI BHABA AND 'THE LOCATION OF CULTURE'

In discussing Said, we've looked at how 'race' is created by the discursive connection of certain signifiers, usually physical characteristics, with determinate signifieds. Now let's ask a tougher question: What is 'ethnicity?' We often use the phrase 'race and/or ethnicity' – so what's the difference? Ethnicity is a less definite category than race, in part because the signifiers of ethnicity are less fixed, less obvious, than those of race. But in some ways ethnicity is a more important category, in our contemporary world, than race. Think about the idea of 'ethnic' peoples globally: the wars in eastern Europe, particularly Bosnia and Serbia, over what ethnicity was the dominant one led to a practice labeled 'ethnic cleansing,' which involved killing all the people belonging to the wrong ethnicity. Ethnic cleansing was a common practice in the twentieth century: the Turkish massacre of the Armenians, the Nazi genocide of the Jews as an 'unclean' ethnicity, the wars between Tutsi and Hutu in Africa, and the wars between Pashtus, Kurds, and Arabs in the area we in the West call the Middle East.

In most of these examples, the question of ethnicity seems to have something to do with national identity. What's the relationship between race, ethnicity, and nationality? How can you tell what nationality someone is, and how is nationality connected to race and/or ethnicity? Certainly in the case of the United States, it's really tough to define what makes anyone 'American' – it's not being born in America, because you can become a naturalized citizen; it's not living in America, because some people who are not citizens live in America, and some American citizens live in other countries. It's not speaking English, because Americans speak all kinds of different languages. So what is it? I'm not as interested in finding an answer here as I am in asking the question: How does anyone define *any* 'national' identity, or racial identity, or ethnic identity – and what are the consequences of those identifications?

I'm asking this because this is a central question in postcolonial theory, and a central question for Homi Bhaba's essay on 'The Location of Culture.' But before we get to that, let's review for a minute some ideas we've already discussed about the notion of identity.

In the humanist model, 'identity' was a pretty easy concept: everyone has a unique identity, a core self which is consistent over time, and which defines the idea of your self. You can name that identity by stating its characteristics: I AM a certain sex, a certain race, a certain age, a certain religion, a certain job or career, a certain family member, etc. I would say that I am a woman, a Caucasian, a 48-year-old, an English professor, a mother of two children. This isn't all that I am, of course, but these words start to provide a framework within which I exist. From a poststructuralist perspective, I am constructed as a subject by all of these discourses: I am a subject within an ideology of gender; I am a subject within an ideology of race; I am a subject within an ideology of age; I am a subject within an ideology of education and work; I am a subject within an ideology of reproduction and family. My ideas about who I am, about what my sex, race, age, etc. mean, come from my position within these ideologies: my sense of self is thus constructed by the ideologies and discourses I inhabit.

This is a pretty bleak world-view, a pretty deterministic one – 'I,' my self, my identity, is merely the product of all the discourses and ideologies that construct me, that interpellate me. But the saving grace is this: I am constructed by multiple discourses, multiple ideologies, all at the same time; there might be 20 or 200 discourses that claim me as a subject. And not all these subject positions are identical: as a mother, I might believe one thing, as a professor I might believe something entirely opposite or contradictory. What this means is that my subjectivity, my identity, is multiple; it is also 'overdetermined,' meaning that my identity is determined not by just one discourse or ideology, but by innumerable ones. This overdetermination – the fact that I can think contradictory thoughts at the same time, the fact that I could simultaneously be determined by my feminist belief in equality and by my maternal belief in having authority over my kids – means that there's no predicting what I will think, say, believe, or do in any specific situation or in relation to any specific idea or issue. At any moment, I can speak from any of my multiple subject positions. And that starts to look almost like having the 'free will' and 'creative uniqueness' we valued so much in the humanist model.

So, if you start thinking of subjecthood not just as constructed, but as multiply constructed, then you have infinite possibilities for what constitutes a subject or an 'I'dentity. And you also have the idea of subjects who do not inhabit unified or stable positions or categories. For example, someone with an African-American father and a Caucasian mother is neither one 'race' or the other, but a mixture of both. Poststructuralist theories of race and ethnicity refer to such people as occupying a *hybrid* position. Such hybridity is inherently deconstructive, as it breaks down any possibility of a stable binary opposition. If race is divided as white/black, or white/non-white, then someone of white and non-white parentage deconstructs and destabilizes these categories.

The idea of hybridity works for all kinds of subject positions: any place where you can cross categories, inhabit two subject positions at once, or find the space between defined subject positions, is a place of hybridity. For gender, an example might be transsexuals; for race, bi- or multiracial people; for religion, people who practice more than one spiritual discipline, or a bricolage of several. And this is where Homi Bhaba wants us to look, in order to think differently about national identities and national boundaries. He begins his essay by talking about 'ethnocentric' ideas, ideas that focus on particular def-initions of selfhood by referring to a unified and unitary set of beliefs, practices, and configurations; he wants to challenge those ethnocentric ideas with the idea of dissonant and dissident and dis-located voices, people whose identities are excluded from these fixed and supposedly stable categories. He names specifically women, the colonized, minority groups, and bearers of 'policed sexualities' as those voices. He focuses on another kind of hybridity, or challenge to stable categories of national identity: the identity of the migrant, the homeless, the refugee, the displaced indigenous peoples.

Bhaba then asks us to think about national identity, and argues that the idea of a homogeneous, stable concept of belonging to a nation is under profound redefinition; he cites the Serbian 'ethnic cleansing' as a horrific example of how far a nation is willing to go, in killing its inhabitants, to produce a unified national identity. The effort to make a defined and unified nation is countered, according to Bhaba, by recognizing the idea of hybridity. He talks about 'imag-ined communities' as the idea of what communities we belong to: our identity is shaped by the 'imagined communities' we claim as our own. A nationality is such an 'imagined community.' Hybridity or transnationalism is a challenge to that idea of a unified 'imaginary community;' hybridity brings up the idea that you might belong to many communities or cultures at once, and transnationalism brings up the idea that identity may not be determined by national bound-aries, either political or geographic.

Bhaba is talking about the twentieth-century world, and more specifically the geopolitical world that was created after the Second

World War, when 'nations' were carved out of territories that had previously been colonial provinces or tribal or ethnic homelands. An example of this is Israel. Israel was created as a state after the Holocaust, and was mapped out on land that had been British Palestine: a territory that had been inhabited by people we now call Palestinians, who had been colonized by the British, suddenly became the state of Israel. That's what the disputes are about in the ongoing Palestinian–Israeli conflict: what 'nation' or 'imagined community' do these disputed lands belong to? The idea of a nation, according to Bhaba, is a fiction, an 'imagined community,' an entity created to forge a new sense of identity, to unite peoples who may have had in common only the fact that they inhabited the same general geographical region.

Again, you can see the problems with 'nationhood' all over the globe, particularly in what the West calls the 'Third World.' Another good example is the Arab states, which were, prior to the Second World War, inhabited by people who practiced the Islamic religion and who were identified as ethnic or racial 'Arabs,' but who imagined themselves belonging to various nomadic tribal communities. In the early twentieth century, these Arab tribes worked together to resist British colonial rule. Eventually the Arab tribes managed to kick out the British, but in order to do so they had to form a 'nation,' like Saudi Arabia, out of all the various indigenous tribes. These tribes, which had existed for centuries, had their own histories and practices and conflicts with each other; uniting them into one coherent thing called a 'nation' has proved to be difficult – as has been true in Afghanistan. Bhaba's question, then, is what holds a 'nation' together, when 'nations' are imagined communities of widely disparate and different peoples? Who, then, speaks for this 'nation' and makes decisions for it in global geopolitics?

Bhaba points to capitalism as a 'connective narrative,' an economic practice that holds the idea of 'nation' together; you can see this every time you see a product stamped with the name of the country where it was made. 'Made in Malaysia' implies that 'Malaysia' is a geopolitical and economic entity, rather than a collection of people of various ethnicities and practices. Nations are thus defined by their economic positions in a global economy, as well as by their political positions in global organizations like the United Nations (UN).

Bhaba is interested in forces and identities that disrupt or destablize the idea of a unified 'nation,' a homogeneous 'imagined community;'

he argues that the concept of 'nation' is built upon the exclusion, or even extermination, of those who are described as not belonging to that nation. When the world is carved up into nations, what happens to those who are excluded from belonging to a nation? What about boat people, stateless people, people whose homes are destroyed and who have no passports to prove that they have a 'nationality?' Where do refugees go when their land is blown up and their nation discards them or their nation is erased from the world map?

Bhaba talks about the idea of the refugee, the displaced stateless person, the nomad, as something that isn't contained within the concept of 'nation,' and specifically which isn't contained within a nation's construction of its history. The idea of a 'nation' is the idea of an entity which has its own history, its own narrative of progress and success: I think of the stories I learned as a child about the foundation of the United States as a 'nation.' Up until recently, that history of the United States left out the histories of the people it displaced, such as the Native Americans and the Mexicans. Bhaba argues that the hybrids, the displaced, the non-nationals, must invent their own 'history,' through art which 'renews the past,' 'refigures' the past as an 'in-between space that innovates and interrupts the performance of the present.'

'The performance of identity as iteration, as re-creation of the self in the world of travel, the resettlement of the borderline community of migration,' is where Bhaba locates the project for those not included in unified definitions of 'nationhood.'[1] This is not just relocating a lost past or reinvoking indigenous cultural traditions, but creating an identity for an 'imagined community' that is not based on geopolitical or economic ideas of 'nationhood.' One important place where this happens, according to Bhaba, is in literature. Where literature has been defined by nationality – English literature, American literature, French literature, Chinese literature – now literature needs to incorporate the transnational, postcolonial, hybrid experience; in fact, this hybridity, this refugee experience, this non-national identity must transform how we think about literature and its relation to nationality. Postcolonial literature, literature by people who can't be identified as belonging to one specific nation, challenges us to think about how we might organize our universities, and our systems of knowledge, so that we don't reproduce the narratives of nationhood and thus silence or lose the voices which are excluded from those narratives.

## GLORIA ANZALDÚA AND 'BORDERLANDS/LA FRONTERA'

Homi Bhaba's idea of 'hybridity' shares the poststructuralist political critique of the binary oppositions that structure racial, ethnic, and national identities with Gloria Anzaldúa's Chicana lesbian feminist analysis of 'the border.' In 'Borderlands/La Frontera,' Anzaldúa describes 'the border' as where two or more cultures, classes, races, ideologies, edge or confront each other. The border is both the space between cultures, classes, races, sexual orientations – the slash – and the place where they meld and mix, where they are both sides of the slash and neither side of it. This marginalized, liminal space is a space of contradictions, a space between and disruptive of defined categories of race, class, nationality, sexuality, and other identity formations.

Anzaldúa's essay is concerned with naming – but not 'mapping' – the multiplicity of identity formations she inhabits simultaneously and contradictorily. She writes in both Spanish and English (in fact, she identifies at least two kinds of English and six kinds of Spanish) to highlight how the politics of language operate within and around the politics of racial, ethnic, national, gender, and sexual identity. She agrees with the (post)structuralist view that language speaks us, and agrees with Bakhtin that the languages we speak define our identity, our cultural make-up, our ideologies, our definition of self. 'Language is a homeland,' Anzaldúa says, '*Un leguaje que corresponde a un modo de vivir.*'[2] She asserts that 'ethnic identity is twin skin to linguistic identity – I am my language.'[3] But those who occupy 'the border,' those who have multiple and conflicting subject positions or identity categories – such as a Chicana lesbian – are '*deslanguadas*' [without language] according to Anzaldúa:

> *Somos los del espanol deficiente.* We are your linguistic nightmare, your linguistic aberration, your linguistic *mestizaje*, the subject of your *burla*. Because we speak with tongues of fire we are culturally crucified. Racially, culturally and linguistically *somos huerfanos* – we speak an orphan tongue.[4]

Homi Bhaba argues for a hybridity imagined and articulated through transnational literatures, but Anzaldúa asks in what language such texts can or should be written. What happens when your language is illegitimate, an unacceptable language?

Anzaldúa's own essay, in English and in Spanish – sometimes translated, sometimes not – embodies her answer to the problem of dominant and subordinated languages and identities. Her concept of '*la frontera*' is a deconstructive place where everything is '*mita y mita*' – half and half. Anzaldúa sees her linguistic mixture, her '*lenguaje mestiza*' as a mode of empowerment, rejecting both sides of a choice structured as a binary opposition in favor of a more multiple version of W. E. B. du Bois's 'double-voiced discourse.' In her text, as in her multiple identity positions, Anzaldua is constantly slipping in and out of two or more worlds and world-views, and she claims this slippage as a form of power: 'Maimed, mad, and sexually different people were believed to possess supernatural powers by primal cultures' magico-religious thinking. For them, abnormality was the price a person had to pay for her or his inborn extraordinary gift.'[5]

## NOTES

1  Homi Bhaba, 'The Location of Culture,' in Julie Rivkin and Michael Ryan, eds, *Literary Theory: An Anthology*. Oxford: Blackwell Publishers, 1998, pp. 939–40.
2  Gloria Anzaldua, 'Borderlands/La Frontera,' in Rivkin and Ryan, eds, *Literary Theory: An Anthology*, p. 895.
3  *Ibid.*, p. 898.
4  *Ibid.*, p. 897.
5  *Ibid.*, p. 890.

## SUGGESTIONS FOR FURTHER READING

Gloria Anzaldúa, *La Frontera/Borderlands*. San Francisco, CA: Aunt Lute Press, 1999.
Bill Ashcroft, *The Empire Writes Back: Theory and Practice in Post-Colonial Literatures*. New York: Routledge, 2002.
Bill Ashcroft and Pal Ahluwalia, *Edward Said*. New York: Routledge: 2001.
Homi Bhabha, *The Location of Culture*. New York: Routledge, 2004.
Henry Louis Gates, Jr, *The Signifying Monkey: A Theory of African-American Literary Criticism*. Oxford: Oxford University Press, 1989.
Ania Loomba, *Colonialism/Postcolonialism*. New York: Routledge, 1998.
Edward Said, *Orientalism*. New York: Vintage Books, 1979.
Robert J. C. Young, *Postcolonialism: A Very Short Introduction*. Oxford: Oxford University Press, 2003.

# CHAPTER 10

# POSTMODERNISM

Postmodernism is a complicated term, or set of ideas, one that has only emerged as an area of academic study since the mid-1980s. Postmodernism is hard to define, because it is a concept that appears in a wide variety of disciplines or areas of study, including art, architecture, music, film, literature, sociology, communications, fashion, and technology. It's hard to locate it temporally or historically, because it's not clear exactly when postmodernism begins.

Perhaps the easiest way to start thinking about postmodernism is by thinking about modernism, the movement from which postmodernism seems to grow or emerge. Modernism has two facets, or two modes of definition, both of which are relevant to understanding postmodernism.

The first facet or definition of modernism comes from the aesthetic movement broadly labeled 'modernism.' This movement is roughly coterminous with twentieth-century Western ideas about art (though traces of it in emergent forms can be found in the nineteenth century as well). Modernism, as you probably know, is the movement in visual arts, music, literature, and drama which rejected the old Victorian standards of how art should be made, consumed, and what it should mean. In the period of 'high modernism,' from around 1910 to 1930, the major figures of modernism literature helped radically to redefine what poetry and fiction could be and do: figures such as Virginia Woolf, James Joyce, T. S. Eliot, Ezra Pound, Marcel Proust, Wallace Stevens, Franz Kafka, and Rainer Maria Rilke are considered the founders of twentieth-century modernism.

From a literary perspective, the main characteristics of modernism include:

- an emphasis on impressionism and subjectivity in writing (and in visual arts as well); an emphasis on how seeing (or reading or perception itself) takes place, rather than on what is perceived. An example of this would be stream-of-consciousness writing
- a movement away from the apparent objectivity provided by *Not* omniscient third-person narrators, fixed narrative points of view, and clear-cut moral positions. Faulkner's multiply-narrated stories are an example of this aspect of modernism
- a blurring of distinctions between genres, so that poetry seems more documentary (as in T. S. Eliot or e e cummings) and prose seems more poetic (as in Woolf or Joyce)
- an emphasis on fragmented forms, discontinuous narratives, and random-seeming collages of different materials
- a tendency toward reflexivity, or self consciousness, about the production of the work of art, so that each piece calls attention to its own status as a production, as something constructed and consumed in particular ways
- a rejection of elaborate formal aesthetics in favor of minimalist designs (as in the poetry of William Carlos Williams) and a rejection, in large part, of formal aesthetic theories, in favor of spontaneity and discovery in creation
- a rejection of the distinction between 'high' and 'low' or popular culture, both in choice of materials used to produce art and in methods of displaying, distributing, and consuming art.

Postmodernism, like modernism, follows most of these same ideas, rejecting boundaries between high and low forms of art, rejecting rigid genre distinctions, emphasizing pastiche, parody, bricolage, irony, and playfulness. Postmodern art (and thought) favors reflexivity and self-consciousness, fragmentation and discontinuity (especially in narrative structures), ambiguity, simultaneity, and an emphasis on the destructured, decentered, dehumanized subject.

But, while postmodernism seems very much like modernism in these ways, it differs from modernism in its attitude toward a lot of these trends. Modernism, for example, tends to present a fragmented view of human subjectivity and history (think of *The Wasteland*, for instance, or Woolf's *To the Lighthouse*), but presents that fragmentation as something tragic, something to be lamented and mourned as a loss. Many modernist works try to uphold the idea that works of art can provide the unity, coherence, and meaning which has been lost in most of modern life; art will do what other human institutions fail to do. Postmodernism, in contrast, doesn't lament the idea of fragmentation, provisionality, or incoherence, but rather celebrates that. The world is meaningless? Let's not pretend that art can make meaning, then, let's just play with nonsense.

Another way of looking at the relation between modernism and postmodernism helps to clarify some of these distinctions. According to Frederic Jameson, modernism and postmodernism are cultural formations which accompany particular stages of capitalism. Jameson outlines three primary phases of capitalism which dictate particular cultural practices (including what kind of art and literature is produced). The first is market capitalism, which occurred in the eighteenth to the late nineteenth century in Western Europe, England, and the United States (and all their spheres of influence). This first phase is associated with particular technological developments, namely, the steam-driven motor, and with a particular kind of aesthetics, namely, realism. The second phase occurred from the late nineteenth century until the mid-twentieth century (about the Second World War); this phase, monopoly capitalism, is associated with electric and internal combustion motors, and with modernism. The third, the phase we're in now, is multinational or consumer capitalism (with the emphasis placed on marketing, selling, and consuming commodities, not on producing them), associated with nuclear and electronic technologies, and correlated with postmodernism.

## MODERNITY

Like Jameson's characterization of postmodernism in terms of the modes of production and technologies, the second facet, or definition, of postmodernism comes more from history and sociology than from literature or art history. This approach defines postmodernism as the name of an entire social formation, or set of social/historical attitudes; more precisely, this approach contrasts 'postmodernity' with 'modernity,' rather than 'postmodernism' with 'modernism.'

What's the difference? 'Modernism' generally refers to the broad aesthetic movements of the twentieth century; 'modernity' refers to a set of philosophical, political, and ethical ideas which provide the basis for the aesthetic aspect of modernism. 'Modernity' is older than 'modernism;' the label 'modern,' first articulated in nineteenth-century sociology, was meant to distinguish the present era from the previous one, which was labeled 'antiquity.' Scholars are always debating when exactly the 'modern' period began, and how to distinguish between what is modern and what is not modern; it seems like the modern period starts earlier and earlier every time historians look at it. But generally, the 'modern' era is associated with the European Enlightenment, which begins roughly in the middle of the eighteenth century. Other historians trace elements of the Enlightenment thought back to the Renaissance or earlier. I usually date 'modern' from 1750, if only because I got my Ph.D. from a program at Stanford called 'Modern Thought and Literature,' and that program focused on works written after 1750.

The basic ideas of the Enlightenment are roughly the same as the basic ideas of humanism:[1]

- There is a stable, coherent, knowable self. This self is conscious, rational, autonomous, and universal – no physical conditions or differences substantially affect how this self operates.
- This self knows itself and the world through reason, or rationality, posited as the highest form of mental functioning, and the only objective form.
- The mode of knowing produced by the objective, rational self is 'science,' which can provide universal truths about the world, regardless of the individual status of the knower.
- The knowledge produced by science is 'truth,' and is eternal.
- The knowledge/truth produced by science (by the rational, objective, knowing self). will always lead toward progress and perfection. All human institutions and practices can be analyzed by science (reason/objectivity) and improved.
- Reason is the ultimate judge of what is true, and therefore of what is right, and what is good (what is legal and what is ethical). Freedom consists of obedience to the laws that conform to the knowledge discovered by reason.
- In a world governed by reason, the true will always be the same as the good and the right (and the beautiful); there can be no conflict between what is true and what is right (etc.).
- Science thus stands as the paradigm for any and all socially useful forms of knowledge. Science is neutral and objective; scientists,

those who produce scientific knowledge through their unbiased rational capacities, must be free to follow the laws of reason, and not be motivated by other concerns (such as money or power).

- Language, or the mode of expression used in producing and disseminating knowledge, must be rational also. To be rational, language must be transparent; it must function only to represent the real/perceivable world which the rational mind observes. There must be a firm and objective connection between the objects of perception and the words used to name them (between signifier and signified).

These are some of the fundamental premises of humanism and of modernity. They serve, as you can probably tell, to justify and explain virtually all of our social structures and institutions, including democracy, law, science, ethics, and aesthetics.

Modernity is fundamentally about order: about rationality and rationalization, creating order out of chaos. The assumption is that creating more rationality is conducive to creating more order, and that the more ordered a society is, the better it will function (the more rationally it will function). Because modernity is about the pursuit of ever-increasing levels of order, modern societies constantly are on guard against anything and everything labeled as 'disorder,' which might disrupt order. Thus modern societies rely on continually establishing a binary opposition between 'order' and 'disorder,' so that they can assert the superiority of 'order.' But to do this, they have to have things that represent 'disorder' – modern societies thus continually have to create/construct 'disorder.' In Western culture, this disorder becomes 'the other' – defined in relation to other binary oppositions. Thus anything non-white, non-male, non-heterosexual, non-hygienic, non-rational (etc.) becomes part of 'disorder,' and has to be eliminated from the ordered, rational modern society.

The ways that modern societies go about creating categories labeled as 'order' or 'disorder' have to do with the effort to achieve stability. Postmodern theorist Jean-François Lyotard equates that stability with the idea of 'totality,' or a totalized system. Totality, stability, and order, Lyotard argues, are maintained in modern societies through the means of 'grand narratives' or 'master narratives,' which are stories a culture tells itself about its practices and beliefs. A 'grand narrative' in American culture might be the story that democracy is the most enlightened (rational) form of government, and that democracy can and will lead to universal human happiness. Every belief system or ideology has its grand narratives, according to Lyotard; for Marxism, for instance, the 'grand narrative' is the idea that capitalism will collapse in on itself and a utopian socialist world will evolve. You might think of grand narratives as a kind of meta-theory, or meta-ideology, that is, an ideology that explains an ideology (as with Marxism); a story that is told to explain the belief systems that exist.

Lyotard argues that all aspects of modern societies, including science as the primary form of knowledge, depend on these grand narratives. Postmodernism, then, is the critique of grand narratives, the awareness that such narratives serve to mask the contradictions and instabilities that are inherent in any social organization or practice. In other words, every attempt to create 'order' always demands the creation of an equal amount of 'disorder,' but a 'grand narrative' masks the constructedness of these categories by explaining that 'disorder' *really is* chaotic and bad, and that 'order' *really is* rational and good. Postmodernism, in rejecting grand narratives, favors 'mini-narratives,' stories that explain small practices, local events, rather than large-scale universal or global concepts. Postmodern 'mini-narratives' are always situational, provisional, contingent, and temporary, making no claim to universality, truth, reason, or stability.

Another aspect of Enlightenment thought is the idea that language is transparent, that words serve only as representations of thoughts or things, and don't have any function beyond that. Modern societies depend on the idea that signifiers always point to signifieds, and that reality resides in signifieds. In postmodernism, however, there are only signifiers. The idea of any stable or permanent reality disappears, and with it the idea of signifieds that signifiers point to. Rather, for postmodern societies, there are only surfaces, without depth; only signifiers, with no signifieds.

## JEAN BAUDRILLARD

Jean Baudrillard, a postmodernist who studies contemporary popular culture, says that commodities – the stuff you buy – are all signifiers. You buy stuff not necessarily because you will use it, or because it gives you pleasure, but because the stuff means something beyond itself – it is a signifier that points to a signified. That signified, according to Baudrillard, is social status, or a subject position within a variety of social codes or models. Thus when you buy a car, you don't buy just any car to drive around in (which would be buying a commodity largely for use value); the car you buy is a signifier of your social position, your income level, your recreational habits, your political/environmental views, whether you have children, etc. So someone who buys a Mercedes is signifying something different from those who buy minivans or SUVs or hybrid gas/electric cars. What is being signified is in fact your position(s) as a subject; according to Baudrillard, identity (subjecthood) is thus a product of the signifiers with which one surrounds oneself, rather than something essential that is unique to each individual, as in the humanist model. Selfhood, for Baudrillard, as for Lacan, is thus always already an alienated position, something defined by externals.

Baudrillard takes this idea of the signifier–signified relationship further in discussing one of his best-known ideas, the concept of the *simulacrum*. He starts with the idea that the signifier–signified relationship is a relationship of a symbol to a notion of 'reality' – signifiers are representations (words, pictures, symbols, whatever) that point to something beyond or outside of themselves, something which supposedly has a reality of its own, regardless of how it is represented. A chair, for instance, just is, whether we designate it by the word 'chair' or by some other signifier; the object with four legs and a seat continues to exist no matter what we call it, or even whether we call it anything. In the world of mass media which Baudrillard studies, however, there is no signified, no reality, no level of simple existence to which signifiers refer. Rather, Baudrillard says, there are only signifiers with no signifieds; there are only pictures of chairs without any real chairs ever being referred to or existing. He calls this separation of signifier from signified a 'simulacrum,' a representation without an original that it copies. Simulacra (the plural of simulacrum) don't mirror or reproduce or imitate or copy reality: they *are* reality itself, says Baudrillard.

In Western thought since Plato, Baudrillard points out, the idea of an original or real thing has always been favored over the idea of an imitation or a copy. This is particularly evident in the arts, where an original painting, or a first edition, is worth a lot of money, while a reproduction (a print, a second or eighteenth edition) is worth very little. In the postmodern world of mass media, however, the original largely disappears, and only copies exist. An example of this is music

CDs: there is no 'original' master version of any music CD, but only thousands and thousands of copies, all identical, all equal in value. Think also about xerox copies: when I make a hundred copies of this typed page, I have an 'original,' but there's no difference between my original and any of the copies – so the 'original' page that came out of my printer is no different from any of the copies that came out of the copier. Mass-mediated forms of communication in postmodern culture revolve around this idea of simulacra, of imitations and copies with no original. This is why Andy Warhol, and his mass produced images of Campbell's soup cans and Marilyn Monroe, is often classified as a postmodern artist.

Simulacra, as signifiers with no signifieds, produce what we know as 'reality,' according to Baudrillard; mass media disseminate these simulacra everywhere, constantly, so that they are unavoidable and inescapable. The simulacra forever being projected at viewers by the mass media provide what Baudrillard calls 'codes' or 'models' which tell us (viewers, consumers) what and how to think, act, believe, buy, desire, hate, etc. Humans in postmodern culture occupy passive subject positions within these codes or models; this idea is similar to Althusser's notion of how ideologies interpellate subjects, but Baudrillard is not following either structuralist or Marxist 'grand narratives' in formulating his theories.

A simulacrum creates a passive subject who takes the simulation as the only necessary reality; a kid playing a race-car video game who then gets behind the wheel of a 'real' car may not be able to tell the difference between the two experiences of 'driving.' The lack of distinction between game and reality is another feature of postmodern culture, one which is illustrated in a host of movies, starting with *War Games* (1983), where a computer simulation of nuclear war threatens to start a real nuclear war, and including all the installments of the movie *The Matrix*. Another example of the collapse between image and reality can be found in such pop figures as Madonna and Michael Jackson, who exist as all image, all 'surface,' all signifier. A humanist investigation of either of these two people would look for the 'real person' behind the glitzy image; a postmodern investigation of Madonna and Michael Jackson would assume that there was no 'real person' behind the image, and that the image itself was all that mattered.

When the image is more 'real' than any other 'reality,' where there is only surface but no depth, only signifiers with no signifieds, only imitations with no originals, Baudrillard says, we are in the realm of *hyperreality*. One of the best examples of such a hyperreality is Disneyland, which is a minutely created 'reality' of things that don't exist in the modern version of the 'real world.' For postmodern theorists, the hyperreality of the created worlds becomes more 'real' than the real world, and in fact highlights how what we have always thought of as the 'real world' is itself a constructed hyperreality.

My favorite example of this is the movie *Wag the Dog*, subtitled 'A comedy about truth, justice, and other special effects.' The movie tells a story about a president who is caught in a sexually compromising situation with a girl scout. To keep this story from being the headline news for the next number of months, the president hires a Hollywood producer to film a 'war' with Albania, and to broadcast that on the evening news as if it were really happening. 'Truth' thus becomes a 'special effect,' something created by visual images in film and on TV; what is on the screen is truer, more real, than what is 'really' happening off camera, and the (passive) viewing public takes it as such. What's funny in the movie, though, is what Baudrillard and other postmodern theorists say is happening all the time. Whenever you watch the news on TV, how do you know that the film clips you're seeing represent something that's 'really' happening, and are not just produced like a sit-com or made-for-TV movie? Baudrillard and others would say you can't know, and in fact there can be no difference between 'reality' and its representation: what's on TV is what is 'real,' is the only reality we can know.

In addition to its focus on the social constructions of 'reality,' postmodernist theory also examines questions of the organization of knowledge. In modern societies, knowledge was equated with science, and was contrasted to narrative; science was good knowledge, and narrative was bad, primitive, irrational (and thus associated with women, children, primitives, and insane people). Knowledge, however, was good for its own sake; one gained knowledge, via education, in order to be knowledgeable in general, to become an educated person. This is the ideal of the liberal arts education. In a postmodern society, however, knowledge becomes functional – you learn things, not to know them, but to use that knowledge. Educational policy today puts emphasis on skills and training, rather than on a vague humanist ideal of education in general.

Not only is knowledge in postmodern societies characterized by its utility, but knowledge is also distributed, stored, and arranged

POSTMODERNISM

differently in postmodern societies than in modern ones. Specifically, the advent of electronic computer technologies has revolutionized the modes of knowledge production, distribution, and consumption in our society (indeed, some might argue that postmodernism is best described by, and correlated with, the emergence of computer technology, starting in the 1960s, as the dominant force in all aspects of social life). In postmodern societies, anything which is not able to be translated into a form recognizable and storable by a computer – i.e. anything that's not digitizable – will cease to be knowledge. In this paradigm, the opposite of 'knowledge' is not 'ignorance,' as it is the modern/humanist paradigm, but rather 'noise.' Anything that doesn't qualify as a kind of knowledge is 'noise,' is something that is not recognizable as anything within this system.

## JEAN-FRANÇOIS LYOTARD

Lyotard says that the important question for postmodern societies is who decides what knowledge is (and what 'noise' is), and who knows what needs to be decided. Such decisions about knowledge don't involve the old modern/humanist standards, such as the ability to assess knowledge as truth (its technical quality), or as goodness or justice (its ethical quality) or as beauty (its aesthetic quality). Rather, Lyotard argues, knowledge follows the paradigm of a language game.

Lyotard argues that knowledge can take two forms: it can be 'science' or 'narrative.' He associates both with ideas about 'language games' from the linguistic philosophies of Ludwig Wittgenstein. A 'language game,' in brief, is any linguistic act (statement, utterance, sentence, etc.). He calls it a 'game' because each linguistic act follows certain rules and uses certain strategies; you might think here about Bakhtin's ideas about heteroglossia, and the different kinds of languages you use in the course of a day in talking to different audiences about different topics and for different purposes. Lyotard talks about 'narrative' as a language game that doesn't need any outside legitimation: when you tell a story, the story simply exists on its own, and you don't need to prove it or footnote it or assert that it's true. We saw a version of this with Foucault's discussion of 'the author function;' he pointed out that authors become necessary when stories do need to be legitimated, when you have to attribute the story to someone who made it up. Some stories, like legends or folk-tales, don't ever need authors; other stories – which

173

are more linked to 'science' than to 'narrative' – do. Lyotard says that no narrative needs legitimation, by definition; if something needs to have an authority behind it to insist that it's true, then it's defined as 'science.' But, Lyotard says, 'science' can never legitimize itself; it always has to refer to narrative (or a narrative) as the authority outside itself that guarantees its truth.

More specifically, according to Lyotard, science depends on what he calls 'grand narratives' – he refers to the grand narratives of the Enlightenment enthronement of reason and Hegel's narrative of the unity of all knowledge. Such grand narratives, or metanarratives, serve as the basis for most forms of knowledge in modern Western culture. The structuralists, for instance, believed in a grand narrative in their attempts to find universal structures in language, in social relations and families, and in myth, which would explain all human behavior at all times everywhere. Such a search for the universal 'truth' is common to both the humanist project and the structuralist project; both depend on the metanarrative that there is something that all humans at all times everywhere have in common, and that it is possible (and desirable) to discover what that commonality consists of. Similarly, the grand narrative of psychoanalysis lies in the premise that the Oedipus Complex, and its related phenomena, are universal, and can explain all human behavior at all times everywhere; the grand narrative of Marxism lies in the premise that material conditions create relations of production, which then determine human behavior at all times everywhere. For Marxists, however, these relations of production which determine human behavior will differ over time and place, as modes of production shift; what is universal in this grand narrative is the idea that modes and relations of production – whatever those might be – determine all aspects of human behavior.

Lyotard's postmodern perspective shows the flaws in these grand narratives, which work to justify and support the broad theories, like structuralism, psychoanalysis, and Marxism, through which the modern (Western) world has come to understand and represent itself. In place of these grand narratives, postmodern theorists like Lyotard propose sets of 'micronarratives' – small stories, small theories, which might explain a certain set of phenomena, but which don't make any claims to universal 'truth.' Such micronarratives would have use value; they could arise from and be applied to specific situations, but none would claim to explain everything, or to explain all other theories, or to be the preferred or dominant framework through which any event could be understood. Post-modern micronarratives thus are multiple – there is one for every situation, rather than one narrative covering all situations – and they are necessarily different and largely incompatible; there's no way to put all the micronarratives together to form one unified coherent idea of how the world, or human beings, operate.

In this sense, postmodernism seems to offer some alternatives to joining the global culture of consumption, where commodities and forms of knowledge are offered by forces far beyond any individual's control. These alternatives focus on thinking of any and all action (or social struggle) as necessarily local, limited, and partial – but nonetheless effective. By discarding 'grand narratives' (like the liberation of the entire working class) and focusing on specific local goals (such as improved day care centers for working parents in your own commun ity), postmodernist politics offers a way to theorize local situations as fluid and unpredictable, though influenced by global trends. Hence the motto for postmodern politics might well be 'think globally, act locally' – and don't worry about any grand scheme or master plan.

There are lots of questions to be asked about postmodernism, and one of the most important is about the politics involved – or, more simply, whether this movement toward fragmentation, provisional-ity, performance, and instability is something good or something bad? There are various answers to that; in our contemporary society, however, the desire to return to the pre-postmodern era (modern/humanist/Enlightenment thinking) tends to be associated with con-servative political, religious, and philosophical groups. In fact, one of the consequences of postmodernism seems to be the rise of reli-gious fundamentalism, as a form of resistance to the questioning of the 'grand narratives' of religious truth. An example of this would be any religious group which censors or bans literary works which question or deconstruct the grand narrative on which fundamental-ist religious beliefs depend; we see this in the Muslim fundamental-ist ban on Salman Rushdie's *Satanic Verses*, and in Christian fundamentalist protests against books like J. K. Rowling's *Harry Potter* series.

## GILLES DELEUZE AND FELIX GUATTARI

A sub-heading no transition (since transitions imply an overall order, a grand narrative that governs the shape of a piece of speech

LITERARY THEORY: A GUIDE FOR THE PERPLEXED

or writing, and gives it coherence and unity) Gilles Deleuze and Felix Guattari are the authors of a number of rather difficult works explaining postmodern ideas, including *Anti-Oedipus*, which (as you might guess) deconstructs and reworks Freud's ideas about the formation of the self and the psyche and the unconscious. In the essay 'A Thousand Plateaus,' taken from their book of the same title, they present the concept of the *rhizome* as a basic structure in the postmodern world.

Deleuze and Guattari start by talking about the idea of 'arborescence,' or the model of the tree as the predominating model for how knowledge operates in the Enlightenment/modern Western world. In this model, a small idea – a seed or acorn – takes root and sends up shoots; these shoots become a sturdy trunk, supported by the invisible but powerful root system, which feeds the tree; from this unified strong trunk come lots of branches and leaves. Everything that is the tree is traceable back to a single point of origin; everything that is the tree is part of a coherent organic system which has grown vertically, progressively, and steadily. This, according to Deleuze and Guattari, is how all humanist/Enlightenment/Western thought has worked, and how all art and literature from that humanist culture has operated.

They want to throw out the model of the tree and replace it with a model of fungus, a *rhizome*. A rhizome is an organism which consists of interconnected living fibers, but with no central point, no particular origin, no definitive structure, no formative unity. A rhizome doesn't start from anywhere or end anywhere; at every point in its existence it is the same, a network of individual but indistinguishable threads. A rhizome is much harder to uproot; an example is crabgrass, which continues to survive no matter how much of it you pull up, since no part is the 'governing' part of the organism.

Another good example of a rhizomatic structure is the Internet, the World Wide Web. Unlike a spider's web, the World Wide Web has no center; there's no place that starts it, controls it, monitors it, or ends it. Rather, the Web is just the interconnection of all the zillions of websites that exist – and which exist only in hyperreality, only in digital form, only as images on a computer screen, and not in any material form. Take any individual website out and the Web still exists, without any impairment of functioning; take out Yahoo and Google and maybe even Microsoft, and the Web will still exist and will still work the same way.

Deleuze and Guattari argue that stories, narratives, literature operate like either a tree structure or a root structure. 'Tree' stories have a beginning, a middle, and an end; they have a linear progression, and tell a story about growth, about achievement, about upwardness. Tree narratives, they say, make the statement 'to be,' continually talking about what is, what becomes, what will be, and what was. Rhizome stories, narratives, literature, on the other hand (or limb) don't have these delimited starting and ending points. They are about a maze of surface connections, rather than about depth and height; they make the statement 'and . . . and . . . and . . .' rather than 'to be,' as they show connections between events and people and ideas without necessarily offering any causative explanations or direction for those connections. Rhizomatic narratives offer what Deleuze and Guattari call 'lines of flight' and 'strategies of deterritorialization,' rather than maps of a territory or terrain.

So. No ending, no conclusion. The writing just s t o p s

## NOTE

1 This list is modeled after a similar list in an article by Jane Flax, 'Postmodernism and Gender Relations in Feminist Theory,' in Linda J. Nicholson, ed., *Feminism/Postmodernism*. New York and London: Routledge, 1990, pp. 41–2.

## SUGGESTIONS FOR FURTHER READING

Richard Appignanesi and Chris Garratt, *Introducing Postmodernism*. New York: Totem Books, 1995.

Steven Best and Douglas Kellner, *Postmodern Theory: Critical Interrogations*. New York: Guilford Press, 1991.

Christopher Butler, *Postmodernism: A Very Short Introduction*. Oxford: Oxford University Press, 2002.

Claire Colebrook, *Gilles Deleuze*. New York: Routledge, 2002.

Chris Horrocks and Zoran Jevtic, *Introducing Baudrillard*. New York: Totem Books, 1996.

Linda Hutcheon, *The Politics of Postmodernism*. New York: Routledge, 1989.

Linda J. Nicholson, ed., *Feminism/Postmodernism*. New York: Routledge, 1990.

Bill Readings, *Introducing Lyotard: Art and Politics*. New York: Routledge, 1991.

Adam Roberts, *Fredric Jameson*. New York: Routledge, 2000.

Barry Smart, *Postmodernity: Key Ideas*. New York: Routledge, 1993.

# CODA: WHAT NOW?

I hope by now you have a better idea of what 'Literary Theory' is than you did when you started reading this book. These ideas, and the conceptual frameworks they offer for understanding how language, subjectivity, gender, sexuality, race, and other constructions of 'I'dentity operate to create the world we live in every day, have been more or less required forms of knowledge in the disciplines of literary studies since 1980, when I graduated from college. Not, of course, without debate and struggle; along with the development and expansion of 'Literary Theory' have come critics who lament the loss of the humanist perspective and the clarity of the New Critical approach to the literary text. While some would prefer that we forget all that we've learned or created in the past decades, others declare that we've done all we can with 'Literary Theory' and are eager to proclaim it dead, or at least dying. The death of Jacques Derrida in 2005 – 39 years after his essay 'Structure, Sign, and Play' – has brought the question into the foreground: Now that we know what 'Literary Theory' is, where is it going and what is its future?

I have no crystal ball; I can't predict what the newest cool kind of theory is going to be. I will predict, however, that 'Literary Theory' is neither dead nor disappearing from the landscape of literary studies. It remains a useful set of tools for analyzing how meaning is made, circulates, performs, and fluctuates in our twenty-first-century culture. 'Literary Theory,' as we've seen, isn't a single static entity; rather, it's like Derrida's description of deconstruction: a set of strategies for reading. As such, these theories have a pragmatic value: they tell us something we need and want to know, something useful. Some of the concern about 'Literary Theory' and its supposed 'domination' of literary studies has come from the fear that the 'Theory' part will become more important than the 'Literary' part – that we'll stop reading 'literature,' stop doing close readings and textual analysis, and stop searching for meaning. I can't imagine this happening; I can't imagine being an English professor, or having English majors as students, who don't continue to value 'the literary' as something important, even as they understand the construction of the category of 'the literary.' It's like the scene in the 1939 movie *The Wizard of Oz*, where Toto pulls the curtain to reveal the man behind the huge green wizard head. Even when you've seen how the machinery creates the illusion, you can still be affected by the 'magic.'

The more pressing question, in my mind, is not whether literary studies will continue to embrace 'Literary Theory,' but whether the university, and the world it helps shape, will continue to embrace literary studies. Universities and their curricula are under increasing pressure from all directions – from tuition-paying parents to salary-paying corporations – to show that they are producing economically viable subjects. The leisured days of the liberal arts may be what is dying, rather than 'Literary Theory' per se. As long as literary studies lasts, though, 'Literary Theory' will remain part of our repertoire of useful tools to understand how – and perhaps *why* – our world works the way it does.

# INDEX